Stop Laziness the Easy Way

A Practical Guide to Unlocking Your True Potential, Boosting Productivity, and Achieving Your Goals Daily.

EMORY LOVE

© **Copyright 2024 - All rights reserved.**

The content inside this book may not be duplicated, reproduced, or transmitted without direct written permission from the author or publisher.

Under no circumstances will any blame or legal responsibility be held against the publisher, or author, for any damages, reparation, or monetary loss due to the information contained within this book, either directly or indirectly.

Legal Notice:

This book is copyright protected. It is only for personal use. You cannot amend, distribute, sell, use, quote or paraphrase any part, or the content within this book, without the consent of the author or publisher.

Disclaimer Notice:

Please note the information contained within this document is for educational and entertainment purposes only. All effort has been executed to present accurate, reliable, up to date, complete information. No warranties of any kind are declared or implied. Readers acknowledge that the author is not engaging in the rendering of legal, financial, medical, or professional advice. The content within this book has been derived from various sources. Please consult a licensed professional before attempting any techniques outlined in this book.

By reading this document, the reader agrees that under no circumstances is the author responsible for any losses, direct or indirect, that are incurred as a result of the use of the information contained within this document, including, but not limited to, errors, omissions, or inaccuracies.

TABLE OF CONTENT

INTRODUCTION	4
CHAPTER ONE	8
CHAPTER TWO DEVELOPING A PRODUCTIVE MINDSET	27
CHAPTER THREE TIME MANAGEMENT STRATEGIES	34
CHAPTER FOUR THE POWER OF HABITS	49
CHAPTER FIVE UNDERSTANDING MOTIVATION	61
CHAPTER SIX MANAGING STRESS AND BURNOUT	70
CHAPTER SEVEN MASTERING FOCUS AND CONCENTRATION	80
CHAPTER EIGHT OVERCOMING PROCRASTINATION	92
CHAPTER NINE GOAL SETTING AND ACHIEVEMENT	108
CHAPTER TEN MAINTAINING MOMENTUM AND CONSISTENCY	123
CONCLUSION EMBRACING A PRODUCTIVE AND FULFILLING LIFE	133

INTRODUCTION

"The secret of getting ahead is getting started." - Mark Twain

Sara leaned back in her chair as the screen of her computer glowed in the dim light of her office. It was late, and the office was quiet, save for the occasional hum of the air conditioner. On her screen was the draft of her job promotion request letter and the cursor blinked at the end of an unfinished sentence.

The proposal had been on her to-do list for weeks. Management had announced the opportunity for promotion and required interested employees to submit a written request outlining their qualifications and why they deserved the role. The deadline was set for today, 5 PM.

Throughout the weeks, Sara had told herself she would start the letter tomorrow, then the next day. She convinced herself there was plenty of time. But days turned into weeks, and the urgency that should have spurred her into action slipped away in a haze.

Now, with only an hour left before the deadline, her proposal was barely half-written. She scrolled through what she had typed and since her mind could not really process the words, She opened a new tab and logged into her Instagram account. She needs that all-too-familiar distraction.

Tom, a colleague and friend who sat in the cubicle next to hers, walked past her office and glanced in. He paused at her door, knocking lightly.

"Hey, Sara, have you submitted your proposal yet?" he asked, holding up his folder.

Sara minimized her browser window and forced a smile. "I'm just putting the finishing touches on it now."

Tom raised an eyebrow, a small smile playing on his lips. "You know it's due in less than an hour, right?"

"Yeah, I know. Thanks," she replied, embarrassed and frustrated.

As Tom walked away, Sara turned back to her screen. She typed a few more words, then deleted them, she tried again but nothing was coming forth. She pushed back again and stared at the clock as it ticked closer to the deadline.

Finally, at 4:59 PM, overwhelmed and defeated, Sara closed the document without sending it. She promised herself she would talk to her boss first thing tomorrow, explain, and maybe it wouldn't be too late.

The next morning, Sara walked into the office with a rehearsed apology and explanation ready. But before she could find her boss, she came across the notice board. Tom had gotten the promotion.

Throughout the day, Sara replayed her actions over the past weeks. She had underestimated the task, overestimated her ability to pull it off last minute, and let her habitual laziness cost her the opportunity.

At her desk, Sara pulled up a new document. This time, it wasn't for a promotion. It was personal. She wrote one question in that document. "How can I change my habits to not only meet my career goals but to live up to my potential?"

If you are reading this book, it means that you are probably just like Sara. You are stuck in a cycle of procrastination and unfulfilled potential. You find yourself consistently putting off important tasks, only to be overwhelmed by the mounting pressure and then you feel disappointment in yourself. Sara's story is a relatable one, and her question is one that I am sure you have asked yourself at some point. Breaking the cycle of laziness and procrastination is a challenge, but you can overcome it with the right mindset and strategies. If you are ready to take control of your life and live up to your full potential, keep reading.

Unlocking the Door to a Productive and Fulfilling Life

I have good news for you. With the right mindset, strategies, and tools, you can break free from the shackles of laziness and unleash your true potential. This book is your guide to doing just that. I am going to provide you with a practical and actionable roadmap for boosting your productivity, achieving your goals, and living a more fulfilling life.

Why You Should Read This Book

If you're feeling stuck, unfulfilled, or simply want to maximize your productivity and achieve more, this book is for you. It's designed to help you:

1. Recognize and tackle the root causes of procrastination and laziness
2. Develop a growth mindset that fosters motivation and resilience
3. Prioritize tasks and manage distractions effectively
4. Cultivate healthy habits that support productivity and well-being
5. Set and accomplish meaningful goals that align with your values and aspirations
6. Embrace a positive and empowering mindset that drives you forward

What Sets This Book Apart

Unlike other books that only scratch the surface or offer generic advice, "Stop Laziness the Easy Way" will provide a comprehensive and practical approach to overcoming procrastination and unlocking your true potential. It combines evidence-based strategies, real-life examples, and actionable exercises to help you implement lasting change.

The Journey Ahead

Throughout this book, you'll embark on a transformative journey that will challenge your limiting beliefs, provide you with practical tools and strategies, and ultimately empower you to overcome procrastination and laziness once and for all.

You'll learn to identify and address the root causes of your procrastination, cultivate a growth mindset that fosters motivation, and develop habits that support productivity and overall well-being.

But this book is more than just a collection of strategies – it serves as a guide to unlocking your true potential and attaining the success and fulfillment you deserve in life. Through real-life examples, inspirational stories, and actionable exercises, you'll gain the confidence and motivation you need to take back control of your time, your goals, and your future.

CHAPTER ONE

"The only way to overcome laziness is through self-reflection and understanding its roots." - **Margarita Tartakovsky**

What is Laziness?

"Lazy? Who, me? Nah, I'm just taking a break...for the sixth time today."

We've all been there - caught between lying on our couch and the nagging voice that reminds us of the mounting to-do list. Laziness is a deceptive cozy companion, that can quickly turn into a relentless enemy, sabotaging our goals and ambitions.

Before we move any further, let me start by debunking a common misconception: laziness is not a character flaw or an indication of weakness. It's a complex psychological phenomenon with roots that run deeper than a mere disinclination to act.

According to Merriam-Webster, laziness is "an inclination not to do work or engage in activities." In simpler terms, it's a reluctance to get stuff done, despite having the capability to do so.

It's important to note that laziness is not the same as procrastination, although the two are often placed side by side like they are cousins, they are not quite the same. Procrastination is the act of delaying or postponing tasks (you know, like binge-watching that new show instead of working on your report), while laziness is more of a state of being - a general aversion to effort and activity.

Think of it this way: procrastination is the excuse you give yourself ("I'll start tomorrow"), while laziness is the underlying reason why you believe that excuse in the first place ("I just don't feel like it").

Identifying Your Triggers

Laziness is something we've all experienced, right? But have you ever stopped to think about what actually triggers that feeling of not wanting to do anything?

Think about it - when was the last time you found yourself procrastinating or just completely avoiding a task or goal? Was it because you just didn't feel motivated or inspired? Or maybe you were dealing with self-doubt or fear of failure.

Sometimes, it's not even about motivation or fear - it's just feeling stressed and burned out. When we're overwhelmed, it's so easy to disengage and avoid our responsibilities. And let's not forget about all the distractions and temptations we face every day.

To overcome laziness, it's crucial to identify the triggers that contribute to this state of mind. This reminds me of my friend Matilda. She had been struggling with being lazy for a while now, and it really became apparent when she started working from home during the pandemic.

Before that, Matilda had a pretty solid routine - she'd wake up, get ready, commute to the office, and her day was somewhat structured. But once she started working remotely, all that structure just went out the window. Can you relate to that? Like, suddenly you have zero boundaries between your work and home life?

For Matilda, it was a perfect storm to trigger laziness in her. Without that rigid schedule to follow, she found herself constantly distracted and tempted by things like social media, her latest Netflix binge, or even just lounging around in her pajamas. And you know how it goes - the more you give in to those temptations, the harder it is to find your motivation again.

On top of that, Matilda was dealing with a lot of negative self-talk. She'd beat herself up for not being productive, calling herself lazy and useless. But that kind of mindset is just a vicious cycle? The more you tell yourself you're lazy, the more you start to believe it and live up to that label.

It is like the analogy of being stuck in quicksand - the more she struggled and berated herself, the deeper she sank into that laziness trap.

But you know what finally helped turn things around for Matilda? She started digging into what was triggering her lack of motivation and procrastination. Was it the endless distractions at home? The lack of a set schedule? The self-doubt and negative self-talk? By identifying those root causes, she could start addressing them one by one.

I'm not saying it was easy - breaking out of those lazy habits is tough! But just having that self-awareness and understanding of her triggers made a huge difference. From there, she could start implementing strategies to overcome them.

Can you see any similarities between Matilda's experience and your own struggles with laziness? Your triggers can be internal (thoughts, emotions, or beliefs) or external (environmental factors or situations). Here are some common triggers that can lead to laziness:

1. **Lack of motivation**: When you lack inspiration or passion for a task or goal, it can be difficult to summon the energy and motivation needed to take action.
2. **Fear of failure or success**: You may procrastinate or avoid taking action due to a fear of failure or a fear of success. These fears can stem from self-doubt, past experiences, or societal pressures.
3. **Stress and burnout**: When you're feeling overwhelmed or burned out, you will disengage and avoid tasks or responsibilities.
4. **Distractions and temptations**: In today's world, we are constantly inundated with distractions, ranging from social

media and video games to streaming platforms. These temptations can easily derail your focus and productivity.
5. **Lack of structure or routine**: Without a steady routine or schedule, it can be difficult to sustain momentum and remain focused on your tasks and objectives.
6. **Negative self-talk**: Engaging in negative self-talk, such as telling yourself that you're lazy or incapable, can become a self-fulfilling prophecy and reinforce laziness.

Procrastination

As I mentioned earlier, procrastination is often associated with laziness, but it's a distinct phenomenon and it stands on its own. According to the American Psychological Association, procrastination is "the act of delaying or postponing a task or set of tasks." It's a voluntary delay of an intended course of action, even though recognizing that the delay could lead to adverse outcomes.

Procrastination can manifest in various ways, such as:

- Putting off important tasks until the last minute
- Engaging in unrelated activities instead of tackling the task at hand
- Overcomplicating or overthinking a task, which then leads to inaction
- Underestimating the time and effort required to complete a task

While procrastination may seem harmless., it can have severe consequences, such as increased stress, poor performance, and missed opportunities.

The Cycle of Procrastination

Procrastination often becomes a vicious cycle that can be challenging to break free from. Here's how the cycle typically unfolds:

- **Task avoidance**: You might initially avoid or postpone a task for various reasons, such as lack of motivation, fear, or distractions.
- **Guilt and anxiety**: As the deadline approaches, you begin to feel guilty and anxious about the unfinished task, which can lead to further avoidance.
- **Last-minute effort**: When the deadline becomes imminent, you finally start working on the task, often under intense pressure and with a compromised quality of work.
- **Temporary relief**: After completing the task (albeit at the last minute), you experience a temporary sense of relief and accomplishment.
- **Reinforcement**: This temporary relief can reinforce the cycle, as you convince yourself that procrastinating "worked out" and that you can repeat the process for future tasks.

Breaking this cycle requires identifying the underlying triggers and developing strategies to combat procrastination and laziness effectively.

Mental Barriers that Cause Laziness and Procrastination

While there are several internal and external factors that can contribute to laziness and procrastination, it's important for you to understand the mental barriers that often make these tendencies worse. Here are some common mental barriers you need to be aware of:

- **Negative self-talk and limiting beliefs**: Engaging in negative self-talk, such as "I'm not good enough" or "I'll never be able to do this," can severely prevent you from having any motivation and drive to work. Similarly, holding limiting beliefs about your abilities or potential can create self-imposed barriers to success in your head.

- **Fear of failure or success**: The fear of failure or success is a significant mental barrier - the fear of failure stems from a desire to avoid disappointment or criticism. The fear of success could be rooted in you being concerned about the increased expectations or responsibilities that come with doing something right.
- **Perfectionism**: While aiming for excellence is admirable, perfectionism can be crippling. Perfectionists often procrastinate or avoid tasks altogether due to unrealistic expectations or a fear of not meeting their own high standards.
- **Lack of self-discipline**: Self-discipline is the capacity to manage one's thoughts, emotions, and actions to attain desired objectives. Without self-discipline, it can be challenging to overcome laziness and procrastination, as these tendencies often require conscious effort and willpower to overcome.
- **Impulsivity and poor self-regulation**: Impulsivity refers to the tendency to act without considering the consequences, while poor self-regulation is the inability to control one's emotions, thoughts, and behaviors. Both of these factors can contribute to laziness and procrastination, as they make it difficult to maintain focus and follow through on tasks.
- **Lack of self-awareness**: Self-awareness entails recognizing and comprehending your thoughts, emotions, and behaviors. Lacking self-awareness makes it challenging to pinpoint the underlying triggers and patterns that lead to laziness and procrastination. This difficulty can hinder your ability to effectively address these tendencies.

Understanding the psychology of laziness and procrastination is the first step towards overcoming these challenges. By identifying your triggers, understanding the cycle of procrastination, and recognizing the mental barriers that hold you back, you can begin to develop strategies and techniques to break free from these limiting patterns.

How Laziness Affects Your Life

Here's the thing - letting that laziness take over doesn't just impact your productivity or ability to check things off your to-do list. Nope, it seeps into all areas of your life like a toxic sludge.

Think about it this way: when you're feeling lazy and unmotivated, it's like you're living in a constant state of "meh." You're just coasting through life, not really putting in the effort to grow, challenge yourself, or strive for something better. Can you see how that mindset could hold you back from reaching your full potential?

On a professional level, laziness can be a total career kryptonite. How are you supposed to crush those goals or snag that promotion if you're always procrastinating or half-assing your work? Your bosses and colleagues are going to notice that lack of drive and ambition, trust me.

Just look at Matilda - she was so consumed by her lazy habits that she started isolating herself and neglecting her friendships and hobbies. It's like laziness became this heavy anchor weighing her down and holding her back from living her best life.

So, let me ask you this: What areas of your life do you feel like laziness might be creeping in and causing some damage? Your work performance? Your personal growth? Your relationships? Or maybe it's impacting your physical or mental health?

The scary part is how insidious and far-reaching the effects of laziness can be if you let it fester. It's kind of like a weed that starts off small and harmless, but if you don't pull it out by the roots, it'll spread and overtake your entire garden before you know it.

Personal Growth and Development

If you want to lead a fulfilling and meaningful life, your dedication to Personal growth and development is essential. Here's how laziness can impede your personal growth:

- **Stagnation and lack of progress**: Laziness often leads to inaction, which can result in you not making any progress towards your goals and aspirations. When you consistently avoid or procrastinate on tasks and activities that facilitate personal growth, you remain stuck in a place for a long time.
- **Unfulfilled potential**: Each of us possesses unique talents, skills, and abilities. However, laziness can prevent you from fully exploring and developing these gifts. By succumbing to laziness, you may never discover or actualize your true potential, and at the end of the day, you will be left with a sense of unfulfillment and regret.
- **Missed opportunities**: Life offers numerous opportunities for personal growth, like acquiring new skills, exploring new hobbies, or pursuing passion projects. However, laziness can cause you to miss out on these opportunities, as you may lack the motivation or drive to seize them.
- **Lack of self-discipline**: Personal growth often requires self-discipline, as it involves consistently putting in effort, overcoming challenges, and pushing beyond your comfort zone. Laziness undermines your ability to cultivate self-discipline and makes it harder to achieve your long-term goals and sustain personal growth.
- **Low self-esteem**: When you constantly fall short of your goals and aspirations due to laziness, you start feeling disappointed in yourself and that feeling leads to low self-esteem. This negative self-perception can become a vicious cycle, further fueling laziness and hindering your personal growth.

Career and Financial Consequences

- **Poor job performance**: Laziness can lead to procrastination, missed deadlines, and subpar work quality. This can have a detrimental effect on your job performance, and potentially jeopardize your job security or opportunities for advancement.
- **Missed career opportunities**: In today's competitive job market, laziness can cause you to miss out on valuable career opportunities. Whether it's failing to apply for a promising job opening, neglecting to network, or lacking the motivation to pursue professional development opportunities, laziness can stall your career growth.
- **Financial instability**: Laziness can directly impact your financial well-being. If you consistently underperform or miss out on career advancement opportunities, your earning potential may suffer. Additionally, laziness can lead to poor financial management, such as neglecting to pay bills on time or failing to save or invest for the future.
- **Lack of job satisfaction**: When laziness prevents you from fully engaging in your work and putting forth your best effort, it can make you unsatisfied with your job. This can further reinforce a cycle of laziness, as you may lose motivation and passion for your job.
- **Damaged professional reputation**: In many careers, your reputation is a valuable asset. Laziness can tarnish your professional reputation, as colleagues, superiors, or clients may perceive you as unreliable, unmotivated, or lacking in commitment.
- **Stunted entrepreneurial ambitions**: For those with entrepreneurial aspirations, laziness can be a significant obstacle. Starting and growing a successful business requires immense drive, dedication, and a willingness to put in the

hard work necessary to overcome challenges and seize opportunities.

Relationships and Social Life

- **Strained personal relationships**: Laziness can make you neglect your responsibilities or commitments within your personal relationships. This can create resentment, frustration, and a lack of trust from loved ones who may feel that you are not putting in the effort required to maintain a healthy relationship with them.
- **Social isolation**: Laziness can cause you to withdraw from social activities and connections. You may find yourself making excuses to avoid social gatherings or neglecting to maintain friendships.
- **Lack of emotional support**: Strong relationships often involve mutual emotional support and understanding. However, laziness can prevent you from being fully present and attentive to the needs and concerns of your loved ones
- **Missed shared experiences**: Relationships often thrive on shared experiences, whether it's creating memories together, pursuing shared interests, or supporting each other's goals and aspirations. Laziness can cause you to miss out on these valuable shared experiences, and thus you feel disconnected from your loved ones.
- **Unhealthy dynamics**: In romantic relationships, laziness can contribute to unhealthy dynamics, such as enabling behaviors or an imbalance of effort and responsibility. This can breed resentment and ultimately undermine the foundation of the relationship.
- **Damaged trust and respect**: Trust and respect are essential components of any healthy relationship. However, laziness can erode these vital elements, as loved ones may perceive

your lack of effort as an indication of disrespect or a lack of commitment to the relationship.

Health and Well-being

1. **Physical health**: Laziness can result in a sedentary lifestyle, not engaging in physical activity, and maintaining poor eating habits, raising the risk of obesity, chronic diseases, and other health problems.
2. **Mental health**: Procrastination and laziness can contribute to heightened stress, anxiety, and feelings of guilt or shame, which can negatively impact your mental well-being.
3. **Self-care**: Neglecting self-care activities like personal hygiene, grooming, or attending medical appointments due to laziness can negatively impact your overall health and well-being.

Education and Learning

- **Academic performance**: Laziness and procrastination can lead to missed assignments, and poor grades, and ultimately hinder your academic success and achievement.
- **Skill development**: Avoiding practice, studying, or engaging in learning activities due to laziness can prevent you from developing new skills and knowledge.
- **Missed opportunities**: Laziness may cause you to miss out on valuable educational opportunities, such as internships, research projects, or extracurricular activities that could enhance your learning experience and future prospects.

Household and Daily Life

- **Disorganization and clutter**: Laziness can lead to you neglecting your household chores, and maintenance tasks, which leads to a cluttered and disorganized living environment.

- **Dependence on others**: Excessive laziness may cause an over-reliance on others to complete tasks or responsibilities, potentially straining your relationships with people.

Myths and Misconceptions about Laziness

I feel like there are so many myths and misconceptions floating around out there, and they can seriously mess with how we view these issues. For example, have you ever heard someone dismiss laziness as just a lack of willpower? Like, "Oh, they're just being lazy and unmotivated." But it's not always that simple, is it? There could be all sorts of underlying factors at play, like mental health struggles, lack of confidence, or even just feeling overwhelmed and burnt out.

It's kind of like when people say, "If you want something done, just do it! Stop procrastinating!" As if it's that easy to flip a switch and overcome that cycle of avoidance and delay. But for a lot of folks, procrastination is a way of coping with anxiety, fear of failure, or even just poor time management skills.

So, instead of judging or making assumptions, we need to have a more nuanced understanding of what's really going on. Because buying into those harmful stereotypes can actually prevent you from effectively addressing your laziness or procrastination issues.

It's like if you've always been told that you're just lazy and unmotivated, you might start to internalize that and believe it's just a character flaw that can't be changed. But what if you reframe it as a pattern of behavior that can be altered with the right strategies and support?

In this section, I'll explore some of the most common myths and misconceptions about laziness and procrastination, and provide a more nuanced and accurate understanding of these phenomena.

Myth #1: Laziness is a Character Flaw

One of the most pervasive myths about laziness is the notion that it is a character flaw or a sign of moral weakness. This belief stems from a simplistic view that laziness is a choice and that individuals who struggle with it lack discipline, willpower, or ambition.

Reality: Laziness is a complex psychological phenomenon influenced by various factors, including mental health, past experiences, and environmental factors. It is not a character flaw, but rather a behavioral pattern that can be affected by underlying issues like depression, anxiety, or low self-esteem. Labeling laziness as a character flaw can be counterproductive and contribute to feelings of shame or self-loathing, making it harder to address the root causes.

Myth #2: Procrastinators are Inherently Lazy

Another common misconception is that procrastination and laziness are synonymous. People often assume that those who procrastinate are inherently lazy and lack motivation or drive.

Reality: While procrastination and laziness can be related, they are distinct issues with different underlying causes. Procrastination can result from various factors, including fear of failure and perfectionism, poor time management skills, or difficulty with task initiation. It is possible for individuals to procrastinate on certain tasks while remaining highly motivated and productive in other areas of their lives.

Myth #3: Lazy People are Unmotivated and Lack Ambition

Another myth about laziness is that lazy individuals lack motivation and ambition. This belief suggests that lazy people are content with underachieving and have no drive to pursue their goals or achieve success.

Reality: Laziness is often a symptom of deeper issues rather than a lack of motivation or ambition. Many individuals who struggle with laziness have ambitious goals and aspirations but face internal or external barriers that prevent them from taking action. These barriers can include anxiety, fear of failure, lack of self-confidence, or environmental factors such as lack of support or resources.

Myth #4: Lazy People are Unproductive and They Accomplish Nothing

A common stereotype portrays lazy individuals as unproductive and incapable of accomplishing anything meaningful. This myth suggests that laziness is incompatible with achievement or success.

Reality: While laziness can certainly hinder productivity and progress, it is an oversimplification to claim that lazy individuals accomplish nothing. Many highly successful and accomplished individuals have struggled with periods of laziness or procrastination throughout their lives. Additionally, laziness often manifests selectively in certain areas or tasks, while the individuals may remain highly productive and accomplished in other domains.

Myth #5: Laziness is a Permanent Trait

Another prevalent myth is that laziness is a fixed personality trait or an inherent part of an individual's character. This belief suggests that laziness is unchangeable and that individuals who struggle with it are doomed to a lifetime of underachievement.

Reality: Laziness is a behavioral pattern that can be influenced by various factors, and it is not a permanent or unchangeable trait. With the right strategies, mindset shifts, and support systems, individuals can learn to overcome laziness and develop more productive habits. Personal growth, therapy, and lifestyle changes can all contribute to breaking the cycle of laziness and unlocking greater potential.

Myth #6: Lazy People are Simply Unmotivated by Rewards or Consequences

Some believe that lazy individuals are unmotivated by rewards or consequences and that offering incentives or imposing consequences will not inspire them to take action.

Reality: While external rewards and consequences may not be the sole solution, they can play a role in motivating individuals to overcome laziness. Many people struggle with laziness due to a lack of motivation or a disconnect between their actions and the perceived rewards or consequences. By establishing clear goals, creating accountability systems, and providing meaningful incentives or consequences, individuals can develop a stronger sense of motivation and commitment to overcoming laziness.

Myth #7: Laziness is Solely a Result of Poor Time Management

Another common misconception is that laziness is primarily an outcome of inadequate time management skills or a lack of organization. This belief suggests that improving time management techniques is the key to overcoming laziness.

Reality: While time management skills can certainly contribute to productivity and task completion, laziness often has deeper psychological roots that cannot be addressed through time management strategies alone. Factors like low self-esteem, lack of motivation, or underlying mental health issues can contribute to laziness and must be addressed holistically.

It's essential to debunk these myths and misunderstandings to develop a more accurate and compassionate understanding of laziness and procrastination. By recognizing the complex psychological factors at play, individuals can then approach these tendencies with greater empathy and develop more effective strategies for overcoming them.

In the next chapter, we will delve into practical strategies and techniques to combat laziness and procrastination, empowering you to help you unleash your full potential and reach your objectives.

Self-Reflection Exercise: Uncovering the Roots of Your Laziness

This exercise is designed to help you reflect on your personal experiences with laziness and procrastination and identify the particular factors that contribute to them in your life. By answering the following questions honestly and thoughtfully, you can obtain valuable insights into the underlying causes of your challenges, which is the first step towards addressing them effectively.

Approach this exercise with an open and non-judgmental mind. The goal is not to criticize or shame yourself but to cultivate compassionate self-understanding. Get a journal or a book before you continue reading.

Part 1: Identifying Your Triggers

- Think about a recent task or goal that you procrastinated on or approached with laziness. Describe the task and the circumstances surrounding it.

Example: "I had an important work project with a tight deadline, but I kept putting off starting it until the last minute."

- What were your initial thoughts and feelings when you first learned about this task or goal? Did you experience any specific emotions (e.g., anxiety, boredom, overwhelm) that may have contributed to your avoidance?

Example: "When I first received the project, I felt overwhelmed by the scope and intimidated by the tight deadline. I also found the subject matter a bit dry and uninteresting, which made it harder for me to feel motivated."

- Were there any external factors or distractions that made it easier for you to procrastinate or be lazy about this task? Describe these factors in detail.

Example: "There were a lot of distractions at home, like my social media notifications, streaming shows, and/or my gaming console, which made it tempting to avoid the project and engage in more enjoyable activities instead."

- Reflect on your internal thought patterns and beliefs surrounding this task or goal. Did you have any negative self-talk or limiting beliefs that may have contributed to your laziness or procrastination?

Example: "I kept telling myself that I work better under pressure and that I could get it done at the last minute. I also doubted my abilities to complete the project well, which made me want to avoid it altogether."

- Did you have any specific fears or concerns related to the task or goal?

Example: "I was really anxious about not being able to meet the high standards my boss expects for projects like this. I kept doubting my abilities and fearing that my work wouldn't be good enough."

- Were there any past experiences or beliefs that influenced your behavior?

Example: "In college, I used to procrastinate a lot on big assignments, and it always ended up being a stressful scramble to get them done at the last minute. I think part of me still believes that I operate best under pressure."

- Did you have a plan or strategy in place to tackle the task or goal?

Examples: "If I'm being honest, I didn't really have a clear plan for how to approach this project. I tend to get overwhelmed when I don't break things down into specific steps, so I just kept putting it off instead of figuring out where to start."

- What were the potential consequences of avoiding this task or goal?

Example: "Missing this deadline could have been disastrous – my job was on the line, and there were financial penalties involved too. But in the moment, it was still easier for me to ignore those risks than face the daunting task head-on."

- How did you eventually approach the task or goal (if you did)?

Examples: "I ended up waiting until the absolute last minute, and pulling an all-nighter to get it done. The quality definitely suffered, and I was an anxious wreck the whole time."

- If you were to do that task again, what could you have done differently to avoid procrastination or laziness?

Example: "Looking back, if I had been more proactive about setting small, achievable milestones along the way, it wouldn't have felt so overwhelming. And being kinder to myself instead of beating myself up over doubts could have helped me stay motivated."

By honestly answering these questions and reflecting on your personal experiences, you will gain valuable insights into the root causes of your laziness and procrastination. These could include factors like fear, lack of motivation, poor time management, perfectionism, or negative self-talk.

Keep in mind, that there's no universal solution since the underlying causes can differ depending on the individual and circumstances. However, identifying these triggers is the first step toward knowing the personalized strategies you can use to conquer laziness and procrastination and reach your goals more effectively.

Note: Do not follow my examples unless they speak for you 100%. Make sure you are writing down your unique experiences and feelings.

CHAPTER TWO
Developing A Productive Mindset

"Your beliefs become your thoughts, your thoughts become your words, your words become your actions, your actions become your habits, your habits become your values, your values become your destiny." - **Mahatma Gandhi**

The Power of Positive Thinking

Just as John Milton says "The mind is its own place, and in itself can make a heaven of hell, a hell of heaven." Our mindset and internal dialogue play a crucial role in shaping our experiences and outcomes. Negative thought patterns and self-limiting beliefs can cause a cycle of laziness and procrastination, while a positive mindset can empower you to overcome them and unlock your full potential.

The way you think about yourself and your circumstances can either be a barrier or a catalyst for change. When we engage in negative self-talk, such as "I'm lazy" or "I'll never be able to achieve my goals," we create a self-fulfilling prophecy that reinforces these beliefs and behaviors. However, through nurturing a positive mindset and reshaping your thoughts, you will break free from these mental barriers and unlock a world of possibilities.

Positive thinking holds significant power that can transform your life in profound ways. It is not merely a matter of adopting a sunny and bright disposition or denying reality; it is a conscious choice to focus on the constructive aspects of any situation and approach challenges with a solutions-oriented mindset.

According to research by Barbara Fredrickson, a positive psychology researcher at the University of North Carolina, positive emotions can broaden your perspective and increase your openness to new experiences and opportunities. This openness can pave the way for the development of new skills, resources, and relationships, all of which can contribute to personal growth and success.

The Benefits of Positive Thinking

- **Improved physical health**: Positive thinking has been associated with a stronger immune system, reduced blood pressure, and a reduced likelihood of long-term illnesses such as heart disease and stroke. Positive emotions and thoughts can counteract the negative effects of stress on your body.
- **Enhanced mental well-being**: People with a positive mindset tend to be more resilient in the face of adversity and better equipped to handle stress and anxiety. Positive thinking has been associated with lower rates of depression and a greater overall sense of satisfaction in life.
- **Increased motivation and productivity**: Positive thinking can boost your motivation and drive, and it can make it easier for you to take action and stay focused on your goals. When you believe in your abilities and approach challenges with a positive attitude, you are more likely to persist in the face of setbacks and achieve your desired outcomes
- **Better decision-making**: Positive thinking can enhance your cognitive flexibility and problem-solving abilities. When you see challenges as opportunities and consider multiple perspectives, you are better equipped to make informed and effective decisions.
- **Stronger relationships**: Positive thinking can foster more meaningful and supportive relationships. If you have a positive outlook, you will often be more empathetic, optimistic, and approachable, which can strengthen your

social connections and promote a more harmonious environment.
- **Increased resilience**: Positive thinking fosters resilience, enabling individuals to rebound from adversity and adjust to change. Positive thinkers are better equipped to reframe setbacks as temporary challenges and maintain hope and determination, which can help them overcome obstacles more effectively.

Signs of Positive Thinking

Positive thinking is more than just a mindset; it manifests itself in our thoughts, attitudes, and behaviors. Here are some signs that you are cultivating a positive mindset:

- You often concentrate on the potential for positive outcomes rather than dwelling on negative possibilities.
- You regularly acknowledge and appreciate the good things in your life, no matter how small.
- You perceive challenges and setbacks as chances for learning and growth, rather than as failures.
- Your inner dialogue is supportive and encouraging, rather than critical or self-defeating.
- You take initiative and actively seek solutions, rather than waiting for problems to resolve themselves.
- You bounce back quickly from setbacks and maintain a positive attitude, even in difficult situations.

Exercise: Identifying Positive Thinking Patterns

Take a few moments to reflect on your thoughts and behaviors over the past week. Can you identify instances where you exhibited signs of positive thinking? Write down specific examples and explore how these positive patterns made you feel and influenced your actions.

The Effects of Negative Thoughts

While positive thinking can be a powerful force for good, negative thoughts can have an equally profound impact on our lives, often hindering our progress and well-being. Understanding the effects of negative thinking is crucial for recognizing and addressing these patterns.

- **Increased stress and anxiety**: Negative thoughts can initiate a stress response in the body, leading to the secretion of hormones like cortisol can result in sensations of anxiety, depression, and other mental health difficulties.
- **Impaired decision-making**: When you are mired in negative thinking patterns, your cognitive abilities can be impaired, making it harder to think clearly and make sound decisions.
- **Decreased motivation and productivity**: Negative thoughts can drain your motivation, making it challenging to maintain focus and productivity, often resulting in laziness and procrastination.
- **Strained relationships**: Negative thinking can foster a critical and pessimistic attitude, which can strain your relationships with others and create an air of tension and conflict.
- **Low resilience**: Negative thoughts can undermine your capacity to rebound from setbacks and manage adversity, making it harder to persevere and achieve your goals
- **Poor Physical health**: Chronic negative thinking has been linked to a weakened immune system, heightened inflammation and an elevated risk of developing chronic health conditions like heart disease and diabetes.

Signs of Negative Thinking

The initial step is recognizing the signs of negative thinking towards addressing these patterns and cultivating a more positive mindset. Here are some common signs of negative thinking:

- **Catastrophizing**: Expecting the worst-case scenario and magnifying the potential for negative outcomes.
- **Overgeneralization**: Making sweeping negative statements based on a single event or experience.
- **Filtering**: Concentrating solely on the negative aspects of a situation while disregarding or downplaying the positive elements.
- **Personalizing**: Taking everything personally and assuming blame or criticism, even when it is not warranted.
- **Black and white thinking**: Seeing situations in absolute terms, with no room for nuance or shades of gray.
- **Mind-reading**: Making negative assumptions about what others are thinking or feeling, without any evidence to support those assumptions.

Exercise: Identifying Negative Thinking Patterns

Take a few minutes to reflect on your thoughts and behaviors over the past week. Can you identify instances where you exhibited signs of negative thinking? Write down specific examples and explore how these negative patterns made you feel and influenced your actions.

Practice Positive Self-Talk vs. Negative Self-Talk

Our inner dialogue, or self-talk, is crucial in shaping our thoughts, emotions, and behaviors. Negative self-talk can reinforce negative thinking patterns and undermine our confidence and motivation, while positive self-talk can uplift and empower us.

Examples of Negative Self-Talk:

- "I'll never be able to do this."
- "I'm not good enough."
- "I always mess things up."
- "This is too hard for me."
- "I'm such a failure."

Examples of Positive Self-Talk:
- "I can do this if I take it one step at a time."
- "I am capable and worthy."
- "Mistakes are opportunities to learn and grow."
- "This is challenging, but I have the skills to overcome it."
- "I am resilient and can bounce back from setbacks."

Exercise: Reframing Negative Self-Talk

Take a few moments to reflect on the negative self-talk patterns you may have identified earlier. For each example of negative self-talk, try to reframe it into a more positive and empowering statement. Write down both the negative and positive versions side-by-side to see the contrast.

Ways to Practice Positive Thinking

Acquiring a positive mindset is a skill that can be developed and strengthened with time. Here are six practical ways to incorporate positive thinking into your daily life:

- Start and end each day by reflecting on the things you are grateful for, no matter how small. Keeping a gratitude journal can help reinforce this habit.
- When you are faced with a difficult situation, deliberately reframe it as an opportunity for growth or learning. Ask yourself, "What can I gain from this experience?" or "How can this make me stronger?"
- Spend time with people who uplift and encourage you, and reduce your exposure to negative influences or toxic environments.

- Engaging in mindfulness activities, like meditation or practicing deep breathing techniques can assist in keeping you grounded in the present moment and cultivate a more positive, non-judgmental perspective.
- Recognize and acknowledge your small victories and accomplishments, no matter how minor they may seem. This can help build confidence and motivation.
- Read or listen to stories of people who have overcome adversity and achieved their goals through perseverance and a positive mindset. Allow these stories to inspire and motivate you.

Exercise: Positive Thinking Challenge

For the next week, commit to practicing positive thinking daily. Each day, incorporate at least one of the six strategies listed above. At the end of the week, reflect on how these practices impacted your thoughts, emotions, and overall well-being. Share your experience with a friend or family member to reinforce your commitment to positive thinking. Make sure you journal at the end of every day.

CHAPTER THREE
Time Management Strategies

Laziness often stems from a lack of direction, organization, and proper time management skills.

Efficient time management is a valuable asset that can elevate your efficiency, alleviate anxiety, and unleash your full capabilities. By mastering the art of prioritizing tasks, eliminating distractions, and developing efficient work habits, you'll be able to make the most of your day and achieve your goals with greater ease. To master time management, we must first re-train our brains.

The main lazy thought patterns that derail productivity include:

- **Procrastination**: "I have plenty of time later to do this task."
- **Avoidance**: "This task is so big and overwhelming."
- **Distraction**: "I'll just quickly check Instagram/Email/News."
- **Lack of priorities**: "This other thing is more important right now."
- **Excuses**: "I'm too tired/unmotivated to work on this today."

Does any of that inner self-talk sound familiar? I'm sure it does because everyone experiences those lazy mental voices sometimes. The key is recognizing them for what they are - obstacles preventing you from achieving your true potential. Don't let them win! Let's look at some specific strategies to prioritize what's important and maximize productivity.

The Eisenhower Matrix: Important vs Urgent

President Dwight D. Eisenhower is famous for his leadership in World War II and as a two-term U.S. president. But he's also celebrated for a brilliant productivity strategy that still gets used today - the Eisenhower Matrix.

The basic idea is to divide your tasks into four categories based on two criteria: Important and Urgent.

- Important AND Urgent tasks (Crises, pressing deadlines, etc.)
- Important but NOT Urgent tasks (Long-term projects, health, relationships)
- Urgent but NOT Important tasks (Many interruptions, meetings, requests)
- NOT Important AND NOT Urgent tasks (Time wasters, trivia, etc.)

Eisenhower's strategy is to:

- Immediately address Important and Urgent items to get them out of the way.
- Schedule dedicated chunks of time for Important but Not Urgent projects. Protect this time fiercely.
- Delegate or minimize Urgent Not Important tasks whenever possible.
- Simply eliminate Not Important Not Urgent time wasters.

Living by the Eisenhower matrix means never procrastinating on crucial tasks, but also never letting yourself get bogged down in a flurry of unimportant busy work. This brings tremendous freedom and focus.

To apply this, go through your to-do list and categorize each item into the appropriate quadrant. Block off time for your Important Not Urgent priorities first. Then you can allow some scheduled time for the distractions you can't fully avoid. Just be ruthless about maximizing Important priorities and minimizing the rest.

The Pareto Principle - 80/20 Rule

Have you ever noticed how a small fraction of your activities tend to produce the biggest results? That's the strange truth behind the

80/20 Rule, also called the Pareto Principle after economist Vilfredo Pareto who first came up with the phenomenon.

The Pareto Principle states that in many situations, 80% of outcomes come from only 20% of causes.

- 80% of a company's revenue comes from 20% of customers
- 80% of complaints come from 20% of problematic employees
- 80% of wealth is held by 20% of the population
- 80% of website traffic comes from 20% of webpages

And here's how the 80/20 rule often applies to work and productivity:

Only about 20% of the tasks and activities you do actually account for 80% of your success and goal achievement. The other 80% of things you spend time on are low-value distractions and busy work.

The good news is, that once you become consciously aware of the 80/20 principle, you can apply it for incredible personal productivity gains. Here's how:

- Use the Eisenhower Matrix to clarify your priorities. Don't let urgent and trivial things disrupt important milestones.
- Time-block your calendar for those 20% activities and do not schedule over this time!
- Say "no" to demands that threaten to steal from that 20% of true peak productivity. Be politely unwilling to sacrifice your most meaningful work.
- Try automating, delegating, or dropping any tasks in the 80% that aren't truly necessary.
- **Live by the motto**: "Only a few things really matter. Give those your utmost."

Batching and Elimination

Once you get clear on your highest priorities through the Eisenhower Matrix and Pareto Principle, it's time to look at specific tactics for getting those tasks efficiently handled.

One powerful method is batching. Batching means grouping similar tasks together into dedicated blocks of time, instead of having them scattered throughout your day.

For example, instead of quickly checking your email every time a new one arrives, set aside two batched 30-minute blocks per day to process all emails at once. That would look like:

- Turn off all email and communication notifications.
- 9:00-9:30 AM: Read, respond, organize, and clear all overnight emails.
- 3:00-3:30 PM: Read all the day's emails before leaving the office.

Using batched time gets you "in the zone" and able to really concentrate without distractions or transition costs.

Other examples of batched task blocking:

- 1 hour to reply to all text messages, missed calls, and social media
- 2 hours of dedicated deep work on a big presentation or report
- 3 hours for churning through administrative paperwork duties
- 1 week per month for home maintenance projects

The magic of batching is being able to fully immerse in an activity without multitasking or distractions. Of course, some tasks still need to be handled sporadically as they arise - like responding to your boss or dealing with something urgent. But any activity that can be grouped into batched blocks, should be.

Along with batching similar tasks, also explore ways to streamline or even eliminate recurring tasks that drain your time. Ask yourself:

- Which tasks, meetings, or approvals can be automated with software or delegated to someone else?
- Which processes have redundancies that could be improved?
- Which recurring tasks could possibly just be...stopped? Are they truly essential any longer?

Scheduling and Planning

One of the foundational pillars of mastering time management and productivity is effective planning and scheduling. Without a clear system for mapping out your priorities and allocating time for them, it's all too easy to get derailed by distractions, procrastination, and the latest "urgent" crisis.

Consistent planning and deliberate scheduling enable you to be proactive about how you invest your precious hours and mental energy. Rather than reactively grinding through each day, you're designing your ideal week in alignment with your deepest goals and values.

Daily, Weekly, and Monthly Planning

If you're someone who feels like they're constantly chasing their tail, struggling to keep up with deadlines and commitments, then listen up because effective planning is the key to regaining control of your life. Let's start with the basics:

Step 1: Set Your Monthly Goals

At the start of each month, take some time to reflect on what you want to achieve. What are your big-picture goals or priorities for the next 30 days? Maybe it's to launch a new project at work, declutter your home, or establish a consistent exercise routine. Whatever it is, write it down and get clear on your monthly targets.

Step 2: Break It Down Into Weekly Milestones

Now that you have your monthly goals in place, it's time to break them down into more manageable weekly milestones. Grab your planner and map out what needs to happen each week to make progress towards your larger goals.

For example, if your monthly goal is to launch a new project at work, your weekly milestones might look something like this:

Week 1: Research and gather requirements

Week 2: Draft project plan and timeline

Week 3: Present project plan to stakeholders and get buy-in

Week 4: Kick-off project and assign tasks to team members

See how breaking that big, daunting goal into smaller weekly chunks makes it feel more achievable?

Step 3: Create Your Weekly Schedule

With your weekly milestones in place, it's time to start filling in your weekly schedule. Block out dedicated time slots for working on those milestone tasks and any other recurring commitments or appointments you have.

Don't just wing it and hope you'll find the time – that's a recipe for laziness, procrastination and missed deadlines. Be intentional about carving out the space in your calendar to make progress on your goals.

And remember, be realistic! Don't overload your schedule to the point of it being overwhelming. Leave some room for unexpected hiccups or emergencies that might pop up.

Step 4: Break It Down Into Daily Tasks

Each morning (or the night before), review your weekly milestones and schedule and map out the specific tasks you need to tackle that day.

For example, if one of your weekly milestones is to "Draft project plan and timeline," your daily tasks might include:

- Research similar past projects for reference
- Outline key deliverables and milestones
- Create a rough timeline and assign an estimated effort
- Review the draft plan and make revisions

By breaking your weekly goals down into daily, bite-sized tasks, you're making them feel infinitely more manageable and achievable.

Step 6: Review, Adjust, and Repeat

Effective planning isn't a set-it-and-forget-it kind of deal. It's an ongoing process of review, adjustment, and repetition.

At the end of each week, take a few minutes to assess your progress. Did you hit your weekly milestones? If not, why? What can you learn from that experience and apply to the following week?

Then, as you head into the new week, adjust your plan accordingly. Maybe you need to re-prioritize certain tasks or milestones. Maybe you need to be more realistic about how much you can realistically accomplish in a given timeframe.

It's important to remain adaptable and adjust your plans as necessary. Rinse and repeat this process each week, and before you know it, you'll be hitting your big monthly goals like a pro.

Using Calendars and Reminders

Now that you know the different ways you can plan your day or week, here are some tools and techniques that can help you stay on top of it all.

Calendars

Your calendar is your best friend when it comes to planning and scheduling. Whether you prefer a good old-fashioned paper planner or a fancy digital calendar app, a calendar will help you map out your days, weeks, and months in a detailed format.

But here's the thing: your calendar is only as effective as you make it. Don't just haphazardly jot down appointments and deadlines. Get intentional about it.

Block out specific time slots for work on important projects or tasks you want to focus on. Color-code different types of activities or commitments to help them stand out.

Reminders

Even the most diligent planners among us can sometimes use a gentle nudge to stay on track, and that is where reminders come in.

Reminders can make a significant difference in keeping track of your schedule.

Create alerts for crucial deadlines, appointments, or tasks that you tend to procrastinate on. And don't just rely on your memory – that's a surefire recipe for forgetting something crucial.

Bonus tip: try setting reminders not just for specific tasks or events, but also for things like taking breaks, drinking water, or stepping away from your desk for a few minutes. A little reminder to take care of yourself can go a long way in boosting your productivity and avoiding burnout.

Scheduling Breaks and Downtime

Look, I get it. You're a go-getter, a high-achiever, and the thought of taking a break might seem like a waste of precious time. But here's the hard truth: If you don't schedule some time to rest, you're headed straight for burnout town.

The Science of Breaks

Numerous studies have demonstrated that taking regular breaks can actually enhance your productivity, creativity, and overall mental well-being.

Your brain is like a muscle. If you flex it too hard for too long without giving it a chance to rest and recover, it's going to get fatigued and start underperforming. By taking strategic breaks throughout your day, you're giving your brain a chance to recharge its batteries and come back stronger for the next round of work.

Scheduling Downtime

First, decide how often you need to take breaks. Some experts recommend taking a short 5-10 minute break every hour or so, while others prefer longer 20-30 minute breaks every few hours. Experiment and figure out what works best for you and your workflow.

Next, actually, block out those break times in your calendar or planner. Treat them like any other important appointment or commitment – because they are!

When those break times roll around, make sure you actually take the break! Don't just power through and ignore them. Step away from your desk, go for a quick walk, grab a snack, or just zone out for a few minutes. Your brain will thank you.

Downtime Isn't Just Breaks

Breaks aren't the only form of downtime you should be scheduling. You also need to make sure you're including regular opportunities for longer periods of rest and rejuvenation.

Maybe that means taking a full day off every week to recharge your batteries. Maybe it's scheduling a weekend getaway every few months to disconnect from work and reset. Or perhaps it's as easy as setting aside an hour each evening to engage in an enjoyable pastime or pursuit that brings you joy and helps you unwind

The point is, if you want to prevent burnout and maintain long-term productivity, you can't just go-go-go all the time. You need to intentionally schedule those longer periods of downtime, too.

Identifying and Minimizing Distractions

One of the biggest productivity killers out there is distractions. I see them as little-time vampires that seem to suck you in and then derail your focus before you even realize what's happening.

It could be the endless notifications pinging on your phone, tempting you to mindlessly scroll through social media for "just a few minutes" (that inevitably turns into an hour-long spiral). Or perhaps it's the YouTube rabbit hole, luring you in with "just one more video."

Whatever form they take, distractions are public enemy number one when it comes to laziness and procrastination. After all, it's pretty tough to get stuff done when your attention is constantly being pulled in a million different directions, am I right?

So, what's the solution? Identifying and minimizing those pesky distractions, my friends.

Identify Your Biggest Time Vampires

The first step is to get real with yourself about what's actually distracting you throughout the day. Is it your phone? Social media? YouTube? Friends? Work you are not supposed to be doing at that time?

Take a hard look at how you're really spending your time, and make a list of the black holes that occur whenever you try to focus Don't judge yourself – we've all been there. Just be honest about what's holding you back.

Once you've identified your main distractions, it's time to...

Cut Them Off at the Source

This is where you'll need to flex your willpower muscles a bit. For each distraction you've identified, come up with a plan to minimize or eliminate its ability to derail your productivity.

For example, if your phone is the one sucking your time, try turning off your notifications (or even putting it on Do Not Disturb mode) during your dedicated work sessions. If social media is your kryptonite, install an app or website blocker to keep you from mindlessly opening those apps.

And if you find yourself getting sucked into YouTube videos or podcasts, set a timer for yourself and stick to those strict time limits. When that timer goes off, get back to work – no exceptions.

Create a Distraction-Free Environment

In addition to cutting off distractions at the source, you'll also want to create an environment that's conducive for you to focus on work. That might mean finding a quiet, clutter-free space to set up your workstation.

It could also mean investing in some noise-canceling headphones to block out ambient sounds or even trying out a website like Brain. fm that streams focus-enhancing background music.

The key is to set yourself up for success by minimizing as many potential distractions as possible in your physical workspace.

But let's be real – even with all these strategies in place, there will still be times when distractions manage to worm their way in and derail your focus. That's just part of being human.

When that happens, don't beat yourself up. Simply acknowledge the distraction, gently bring your attention back to the task at hand, and keep pushing forward. It's a practice, not a perfect science.

Saying "No" to Non-Essential Tasks

Taking on too many non-essential tasks and commitments is a laziness enabler. We've all been there it is a familiar feeling of being overwhelmed and stretched too thin because you're juggling a million different plates at once.

The harsh truth? A lot of that busyness and stress is self-inflicted. We say "yes" to things we probably should have declined, thus overcommitting ourselves and spreading our focus too thin in the process.

But here's the thing: when you're trying to be productive and overcome laziness, learning to say "no" to non-essential tasks is absolutely crucial. Let me explain...

At the end of the day, we all have the same 24 hours in a day, right? The key to making the most of that time is prioritizing the tasks and commitments that actually move the needle for your goals and well-being.

That might mean focusing on your high-impact work projects and enjoying meaningful time with family and friends or carving out space for self-care activities that recharge your batteries. Whatever it is, those should be your top priorities.

Everything else? Well, those are prime candidates for the "no" treatment.

How to (Politely) Say "No"

Saying "no" can be tough, particularly if you're a people-pleaser by nature. But if you want to overcome laziness and be more productive, you have to get comfortable with declining non-essential tasks and requests.

You don't have to be a jerk about it. There are polite, tactful ways to say "no" without burning bridges or making people feel rejected.

For example, you could say something like:

"Thanks so much for thinking of me for this, but I'm actually at capacity with my current commitments right now. I'll have to respectfully decline."

Or:

"I really appreciate you asking, but I need to prioritize a few other important projects over the next few weeks. Perhaps we could revisit this later?"

See? Simple, straightforward, and no hard feelings.

Now, I know what you might be thinking: "But what if it's my boss or a higher-up asking me to take something on? I can't exactly say 'no' in that situation!"

Fair point. In cases like that, my advice would be to have an honest conversation about priorities and boundaries. Explain that you're already at capacity with your existing workload, and ask for guidance on what should take precedence.

The key is to approach it collaboratively and come to a mutual understanding, rather than just saying "no" outright.

Delegating and Outsourcing

For a lot of us, the idea of handing off tasks or projects to someone else can feel a bit... uncomfortable. Maybe you're someone who likes to be in control and you struggle to relinquish the reins. Or perhaps you've just gotten so used to doing everything yourself that the thought of delegating feels foreign and awkward.

You have to get comfortable with delegating and outsourcing certain tasks and responsibilities if you want to skip the circle of laziness and procrastination. Period.

The first step is to adopt the right mindset around delegation. Too often, we view it as a sign of weakness or inability – a last resort for when we simply can't handle something ourselves.

But that's the wrong way to look at it. Instead, think of delegation as a strategic tool for maximizing your productivity and impact.

After all, you only have so much time, and energy in a given day, right? By delegating lower-priority tasks to others, you're freeing up your precious time and mental space to focus on your highest-leverage activities – the things that only you can do, and the things that will have the biggest impact.

It's not about being lazy or incapable. It's about being intentional with how you allocate your limited resources for maximum efficiency.

What (and Who) to Delegate

The question you're probably now is "What tasks or responsibilities should I actually delegate, and to whom?"

The simple answer? Anything that isn't an essential, high-priority item for you should be on the table for delegation.

Maybe that's administrative tasks like scheduling, data entry, or inbox management. Perhaps it's more tactical work like research, writing, or design. Or it could be personal errands or chores that are eating into your productivity time.

As for who to delegate to, you've got a few options:

- Teammates or subordinates (if you have a team)
- Freelancers or virtual assistants
- Delegating certain tasks to friends or family members
- Outsourcing to services or agencies

The key is to take a hard look at where you're currently spending your time, identify the areas that could be handled by someone else, and then start exploring your delegation options.

One final word of advice when it comes to delegation: don't be a micro-manager. Nothing will undermine your productivity gains faster than constantly looking over someone's shoulder or nitpicking every little detail.

When you delegate a task, be clear about the desired outcome and any essential requirements, but then give the person you've delegated the autonomy and space to figure out the "how" for themselves.

Trust that you've chosen the right person for the job, provide the necessary context and resources, and then step back and let them work their magic. Only step in if they veer wildly off course or there are clear red flags.

Otherwise, allow yourself to truly offload that mental burden and free up your focus. That's the whole point of delegation, after all!

Just implementing one or two of these strategies can start helping you move in a big way when it comes to overcoming procrastination and laziness.

So pick a starting point that resonates with you, and start putting it into practice. Maybe it's doing a distraction audit and cutting off your biggest time vampires at the source. Or perhaps you're feeling fired up about learning to say "no" more often to requests that don't serve you.

Whichever strategy you choose to focus on first, stick with it and remain consistent. Habits take time to form, but trust me – the benefits of improved efficiency and tangible results make the effort completely worthwhile.

So what are you waiting for? The path to overcoming laziness starts today, my friends. Now get out there and start putting in the work!

CHAPTER FOUR
The Power Of Habits

We are what we do repeatedly. This famous quote by Aristotle highlights the pivotal role of habits in molding our lives... Habits are the foundation upon which our daily routines, productivity levels, and overall success are built. Understanding how habits are formed is essential whether you want to change a bad habit or develop a new positive one.

Habits are instinctive actions that are activated by particular stimuli in our surroundings. These cues can be anything from a particular time of day to a certain location, or even an emotional state. Once it's triggered, the habit unfolds almost effortlessly, without much conscious thought or willpower required.

The beauty of habits lies in their efficiency. Our brains are hardwired to automate recurring patterns and free up mental resources for more complex tasks. Now imagine if you had to consciously think about every single action involved in getting dressed or brushing your teeth each morning – it would be exhausting! Habits allow us to streamline these routine activities, and conserve our mental energy for more demanding challenges.

However, habits can work both for and against us. Just as we can develop habits that enhance our productivity and well-being, we can also fall victim to habits that hold us back, such as procrastination, unhealthy eating patterns, or mindless browsing on our devices.

Understanding how habits form is crucial for unlocking our full potential and using that knowledge to our benefit. By mastering the art of habit formation, we have the ability to change our lives gradually, one step at a time.

Understanding Habit Formation

To truly grasp the power of habits, we must first understand the process by which they are formed. Habits are created through a loop consisting of four distinct stages:

- **Cue**

This is the trigger that sets the habit in motion. It could refer to a particular time, place, mood, or preceding activity.

- **Craving**

Once the cue is encountered, we experience a craving or urge to engage in the habit. This craving can be physical, emotional, or intellectual in nature.

- **Response**

This is the actual behavior or habit itself, triggered by the cue and fueled by the craving.

- **Reward**

The reward functions as a form of positive reinforcement that reinforces the habit loop, increasing the likelihood of the same behavior recurring in the future.

This habit loop becomes deeply ingrained through repetition, and it eventually becomes automatic and requires minimal conscious effort. The more we repeat the loop, the stronger the neural pathways associated with the habit become, making it increasingly difficult to break or modify.

Understanding this loop is crucial for both breaking unwanted habits and cultivating the new ones you desire. By understanding the triggers that initiate our routines and the incentives that support them, we can effectively manage and influence our behaviors.

The Habit Loop

To illustrate the habit loop in action, let's examine a common example: you are snacking while watching television.

- **Cue**: You settle on the couch after a long day and turn on the TV.
- **Craving**: As the familiar sights and sounds of your favorite show begin, you experience a craving for something to munch on, perhaps out of boredom or as a way to relax.
- **Response**: You reach for a bag of chips or a box of cookies, automatically and without much thought.
- **Reward**: The salty or sweet taste of the snack, combined with the comfort of watching TV, provides a sense of pleasure and relaxation, reinforcing the habit loop.

Over time, this cycle becomes so deeply ingrained that the mere act of turning on the TV can trigger an almost predictable response - picking up a snack - even if you're not particularly hungry.

By breaking down this loop and understanding its components, you can begin to disrupt or modify the habit. For example, you could remove the cue by avoiding watching TV while snacking, or you could introduce a new, healthier response, such as reaching for a bowl of fresh fruit instead of chips.

Replacing Bad Habits with Good Ones

While breaking bad habits is certainly challenging, it's often easier to replace them with new, more positive ones. This approach leverages the power of habit formation while redirecting it towards productive and beneficial behaviors.

When attempting to replace a bad habit, it's essential to identify the cue and the underlying craving or reward that drives the behavior. Once you understand these elements, you can introduce a new, healthier response that satisfies the same craving but leads to a more desirable outcome.

For example, if you're trying to break the habit of snacking while watching TV, you could introduce a new response, such as doing light stretches or engaging in a brief exercise routine during commercial breaks. This new behavior taps into the same craving for relaxation and comfort but provides a healthier reward in the form of physical activity and endorphin release.

Another effective strategy for replacing bad habits is to stack a new, desired behavior onto an existing habit you already have. This technique, known as "habit stacking," leverages the momentum and routine of an established habit to introduce a new one.

Suppose you want to develop the habit of reading more books. You could stack this new behavior onto your existing habit of drinking your morning coffee by committing to reading a few pages or chapters while enjoying your daily cup.

When you piggyback on an existing habit, you create a natural cue and reinforce the new behavior through the familiar routine and rewards associated with the original habit. Over time, the new habit becomes deeply ingrained, and the stacking process can be repeated to introduce additional positive behaviors.

Keep in mind that substituting negative behaviors with positive ones takes time, determination, and a readiness to try different approaches. It's essential to be kind to yourself and celebrate little triumphs along the way, as each step forward moves you nearer to your objectives and a more satisfying life.

Creating a Morning Routine

One of the most powerful tools to help you overcome laziness and be more productive is a well-crafted morning routine. How you start your day establishes the mood for the rest of it and can profoundly impact your mindset, energy levels, and overall effectiveness.

A morning routine serves several important functions:

- **It establishes a consistent pattern**

By following the same series of actions each morning, you create a sense of structure and predictability that helps anchor your day.

- **It allows you to prioritize important tasks**

A well-designed morning routine ensures that you tackle your most important tasks and activities before the distractions and demands of the day take over.

- **It cultivates positive habits**

Remember that in the morning, you can integrate exercise, meditation, or journaling into your routine.

- **It provides a sense of control**

In a world that often feels chaotic and overwhelming, a morning routine gives you a sense of control over your life and how you spend your time.

- **It boosts productivity and focus**

By beginning your day with a definite strategy and a feeling of direction, you are more prepared to approach your tasks with concentration and productivity.

Developing an effective morning routine is a highly personal endeavor, as everyone's preferences, goals, and circumstances are unique. However, there are some universal principles and exercises that can guide you in creating a routine that works for you.

The Importance of a Good Start

The way you start your day can have a profound impact on your overall productivity, mindset, and well-being. A chaotic, rushed, and disorganized morning can leave you feeling frazzled, unfocused, and ill-prepared to tackle the challenges ahead.

On the other hand, a well-structured morning routine can set the tone for a successful and productive day. By establishing a consistent pattern and prioritizing important tasks and habits, you can start your day with a sense of purpose, control, and accomplishment.

One of the key benefits of a good morning routine is that it allows you to tackle your most important tasks and activities before the distractions and demands of the day take over. Whether it's tackling a high-priority project, engaging in exercise, or simply taking time for quiet reflection, a morning routine ensures that these crucial activities get the attention they deserve.

Moreover, a morning routine can help cultivate positive habits and promote overall well-being. By incorporating practices like meditation, journaling, or healthy meal preparation, you're setting yourself up for success throughout the day, both mentally and physically.

A carefully planned morning schedule can act as an effective tool for boosting productivity helping you maximize your focus, energy, and effectiveness from the moment you wake up.

How To Create an Effective Morning Routine

To help you develop a morning routine that works for you, let's walk through a step-by-step exercise:

- **Determine your ideal wake-up time**

Identify the time you need to wake up to ensure you have enough time for your morning routine without feeling rushed. Consider factors like your commute, family obligations, and personal preferences.

- **Establish your non-negotiables**

What are the essential elements you want to include in your morning routine? Write them down in your journal. Don't think it's just write as many as possible.

- **Break it down into manageable steps**

Once you've identified your non-negotiable elements, break them down into specific, actionable steps. For example, if exercise is a priority, decide on the type of workout, duration, and whether you'll need any equipment or preparation.

- **Create a timeline**

Assign a realistic time allocation for each step in your routine, and make sure to factor in potential delays or distractions. This will help you stay on track and ensure you don't underestimate the time required.

- **Prioritize your steps**

Arrange the steps in your routine based on importance and the time of day that works best for each activity. For example, you may want to tackle your most mentally demanding tasks early when your focus is sharpest.

- **Build in buffers**

Leave some room between steps to account for unexpected delays or emergencies. This will help prevent your routine from feeling rushed or overwhelming.

- **Start small and build up**

If you're new to having a structured morning routine, start with just a few key elements and gradually add more as you become accustomed to the process.

- **Plan for flexibility**

While consistency is important, remember that life can be unpredictable. Have a backup plan or simplified version of your routine for days when unexpected circumstances arise.

- **Track and adjust**

Keep a journal or log to monitor how your morning routine is working for you. Regularly evaluate what is performing effectively and what requires adjustments or elimination.

Remember, creating an effective morning routine is an iterative process. It may take some trial and error to find the perfect combination of activities and timing that works best for your lifestyle and goals. Be patient with yourself, and don't be afraid to make adjustments as needed.

Examples of Productive Morning Routines

To provide some inspiration and guidance, let's explore a few examples of productive morning routines:

Michael's Routine

- 5:30 AM: Wake up and practice mindfulness or meditation (10 minutes)
- 5:40 AM: Drink a glass of water and review your daily goals (5 minutes)
- 5:45 AM: Light exercise (20 minutes)
- 6:05 AM: Shower and get ready for the day (25 minutes)
- 6:30 AM: Prepare and enjoy a nutritious breakfast (30 minutes)
- 7:00 AM: Review your schedule and prioritize tasks for the day (15 minutes)
- 7:15 AM: Begin your workday or commute

Marie's Routine

- 6:30 AM: Wake up and practice deep breathing exercises (5 minutes)
- 6:35 AM: Journaling and reflection (30 minutes)
- 7:05 AM: Prepare a healthy smoothie or light breakfast (15 minutes)
- 7:20 AM: Review your goals and plan for the day (10 minutes)

- 7:30 AM: Get ready for the day (30 minutes)
- 8:00 AM: Begin your workday or commute

Mina's Routine

- 6:00 AM: Wake up and listen to an educational podcast or audiobook while getting ready (30 minutes)
- 6:30 AM: Prepare a nutritious breakfast and pack a healthy lunch (30 minutes)
- 7:00 AM: Review and respond to important emails or messages (30 minutes)
- 7:30 AM: Light exercise or stretching (20 minutes)
- 7:50 AM: Final preparations and begin your commute or workday

Remember, these are just examples to provide inspiration. The key is to tailor your morning routine to your specific goals, preferences, and lifestyle.

Customizing Your Morning Routine

It's important to note that although the given examples can be used as a foundation, it's crucial to tailor your morning schedule to fit your individual situation, aspirations, and choices. It's often ineffective to use a one-size-fits-all approach for personal routines since everyone has varying priorities, energy levels, and obligations.

To create a truly effective morning routine, consider the following factors:

- **Your chronotype**

Are you a natural early bird or a night owl? Understanding your circadian rhythms and energy patterns can help you determine the optimal timing for different activities in your routine.

- **Your goals and priorities**

What are the most important things you want to accomplish or focus on in your life right now? Your morning routine should reflect and support these goals, whether it's improving your health, advancing your career, or pursuing a personal passion.

- **Your lifestyle and obligations**

Do you have a long commute, family responsibilities, or other time constraints? Factor these into your routine to ensure it's realistic and sustainable.

- **Your personal preferences**

Some people excel with structure and routine, while others thrive with more flexibility. Tailor your morning to align with your preferences.

- **Your energy levels**

Pay attention to when you feel most energized and focused throughout the day, and prioritize your most demanding tasks or activities accordingly.

- **Your living situation**

If you share living space with others, consider how your morning routine might impact or be impacted by their schedules and routines.

Once you've considered these factors, experiment with different combinations of activities and timings until you find a routine that feels natural, energizing, and conducive to your productivity and well-being.

Remember, your morning routine should bring joy and empowerment, not feel like a rigid set of rules or obligations. Regularly evaluate and adjust your routine as your circumstances or priorities change, and don't be afraid to shake things up if you find yourself stuck in a rut.

Optimizing Your Work Environment

While a well-crafted morning routine sets the stage for a productive day, optimizing your work environment is equally crucial for sustaining that productivity throughout the day. Your physical environment can significantly affect your focus, energy levels, and overall effectiveness.

Workspace Organization

A cluttered, disorganized workspace can be a major cause of stress and distraction, and it can impede your ability to concentrate and work efficiently. While a clean, organized environment can promote a sense of calm and clarity, allowing you to focus on the tasks at hand.

If you want to archive the latter, start by decluttering your workspace. Remove any unnecessary items or materials that contribute to visual clutter. Invest in organizational tools like file folders, trays, or storage containers to keep your desk tidy and everything within easy reach.

Next, consider the layout of your workspace. Arrange your desk and chair in a way that promotes good posture and ergonomics to reduce the risk of physical discomfort or strain. Keep frequently used items within easy reach to minimize unnecessary movements or stretching.

Finally, customize your workspace with objects that bring you inspiration or motivation. This could be a framed quote, a cherished photograph, or a small plant – anything that creates a positive and energizing atmosphere conducive to productivity.

Minimizing Distractions

In today's 'online' world, distractions are everywhere – from email notifications and social media alerts to online videos and articles. While some distractions are unavoidable, it's essential that you take some steps to minimize their impact on your productivity.

Start by identifying your primary sources of distraction. Do you find yourself constantly checking your phone or getting sidetracked by online rabbit holes? Once you've pinpointed the culprits, implement strategies to mitigate their impact.

Consider utilizing website blockers or app limiters to restrict access to distracting sites or applications during designated work periods. Disable notifications for non-essential apps or services, and set your communication tools (email, messaging apps, etc.) to "do not disturb" mode when you need to concentrate on focused work.

If external noise or activity is a significant distraction, invest in noise-cancelling headphones or consider finding a quieter workspace, if possible.

Finally, practice mindfulness and self-awareness. When you find yourself becoming distracted, gently redirect your attention back to the task at hand. Over time, this mental muscle will become stronger, and it improves your ability to maintain focus and productivity.

CHAPTER FIVE
Understanding Motivation

Motivation is the inner force that pushes us forward, fuels our actions, and inspires us to push beyond our limitations. Whether you're striving to launch a successful business, excel in your career, or simply cultivate a healthier lifestyle, harnessing the power of motivation is crucial.

However, motivation isn't a steady force; it responds to internal and external factors in our surroundings. To achieve long-term success, it's important to grasp the essence of motivation and create methods to foster and maintain it, even when dealing with obstacles and disappointments.

Intrinsic vs. Extrinsic Motivation

To truly leverage the power of motivation, it's crucial to grasp the difference between intrinsic and extrinsic motivation. Intrinsic motivation stems from within – it's the inherent inclination to participate in an activity for its own sake, propelled by personal interest, enjoyment, or a sense of purpose. On the other hand, extrinsic motivation stems from external sources, such as rewards, recognition, or the avoidance of punishment.

Though both types of motivation can be effective temporarily, intrinsic motivation is generally considered more powerful and sustainable in the long run. When we're intrinsically motivated, we're more likely to persist in the face of obstacles, experience greater satisfaction and fulfillment, and maintain our commitment even when external rewards or recognition are absent.

However, it's important to understand that intrinsic and extrinsic motivation can exist together and work well with each other rather than being mutually exclusive. For example, while you may initially pursue a goal due to external factors (e.g., earning a higher salary), over time, as you develop a genuine interest or passion for the activity, intrinsic motivation can take root and become the driving force.

The key is to cultivate and nurture your intrinsic motivation by aligning your goals and pursuits with your core values, interests, and personal growth. When you find activities that resonate with your authentic self, the motivation to persist and excel becomes self-sustaining.

Finding Your "Why"

One of the most powerful tools for cultivating intrinsic motivation is to identify and connect with your "why" – the deeper purpose or reason behind your goals and aspirations. Your "why" serves as a guiding light, a source of inspiration that transcends surface-level desires or external rewards.

To uncover your "why," find a place to self-reflect and ask yourself these probing questions:

- What truly matters to me in life?
- What legacy do I want to leave behind?
- How can my pursuits positively impact others or contribute to a greater cause?
- What values or principles are most important to me, and how can my goals align with them?

By connecting your goals to a deeper sense of purpose, you create a wellspring of motivation that can sustain you through even the most challenging times. Your "reason for doing something" becomes the anchor that keeps you rooted and concentrated, even when external circumstances or rewards shift.

Staying Motivated in the Long Term

While cultivating intrinsic motivation is crucial, it's also important to recognize that motivation is not a constant state; it fluctuates, and there will be times when your drive and enthusiasm wane. Anticipating and preparing for these moments is key to maintaining progress and avoiding prolonged periods of laziness or procrastination.

One effective strategy is to create a motivation toolkit – a collection of resources, reminders, and techniques that you can draw upon when your motivation starts to flag. This toolkit might include:

- Inspirational quotes, books, or podcasts that resonate with your "why"
- Visual reminders of your goals and accomplishments (vision boards, progress charts, etc.)
- Having a strong support system of friends, family, or mentors who can offer support and assist you to stay responsible
- Techniques for reframing negative thought patterns and cultivating a growth mindset
- Rewards or treats that you can enjoy after achieving milestones or overcoming challenges

By having this toolkit at your disposal, you can proactively address those moments when your motivation dips and reignite your inner drive before it fades completely.

Additionally, it's essential to embrace the flow of motivation as a natural part of the journey. Rather than berating yourself for temporary lapses, approach them with curiosity and self-compassion. Reflect on the factors that may have contributed to the dip, and adjust your strategies accordingly.

Keep in mind that motivation is not something finite; rather, it's like a muscle that can be developed and nurtured over time through continuous effort and self-reflection.

Cultivating Self-Discipline

While motivation provides the spark that ignites action, self-discipline is the sustaining force that pushes us forward, even in the face of resistance, distractions, or momentary lapses in motivation. Self-discipline is the ability to consistently act in alignment with our goals and values, regardless of our fleeting emotions or circumstances.

Cultivating self-discipline is a journey of personal growth and self-mastery, one that requires a combination of commitment, habit formation, and resilience. It's about training our minds and bodies to consistently choose the actions and behaviors that align with our long-term objectives, even when we are tempted by immediate gratification.

The Power of Commitment

The foundation of self-discipline is unwavering commitment – a resolute decision to pursue your goals and follow through on your intentions, no matter what obstacles or challenges arise. Without this deep-rooted commitment, it becomes all too easy to falter or abandon our pursuits at the first sign of resistance or difficulty.

Commitment is not merely a mental exercise; it's a visceral, emotional decision that resonates at the core of our being. It's the recognition that our goals and aspirations are non-negotiable, and we are willing to do whatever it takes to achieve them.

To cultivate this level of commitment, it's essential to connect with your "why" – the deeper purpose or motivation that underpins your goals. When your pursuits are rooted in something profoundly meaningful and aligned with your values, the commitment to see them through becomes unshakable.

Furthermore, it can be beneficial to partake in symbolic gestures that strengthen your determination and underscore the significance of your choice. This could involve writing a personal manifesto, sharing your goals and intentions with loved ones, or even performing a symbolic gesture (e.g. burning a representation of your old habits or limitations).

How to Build Self-discipline

Just like building your physical muscle requires consistent training, developing self-discipline is an ongoing process that requires practice and increasing challenges. This exercise will help you lay the foundation for lasting self-discipline.

Part 1: Define Your Priorities

Self-discipline is easier to muster when you're deeply committed to something meaningful. Reflect on these questions:

- What are your core values in life? (Examples: Growth, health, service, integrity)
- What is your biggest goal or aspiration right now?
- How will cultivating more self-discipline help you live according to your values and achieve your goal?

Write down 1-3 sentences summarizing why self-discipline is invaluable for you right now. Let this motivate you.

Part 2: Start Small, Build Consistency

The key is establishing a consistent baseline before adding intensity. Choose 1-2 small disciplined habits to practice daily:

- Making your bed each morning
- Doing 10 body-weight squats
- Drinking a glass of water first thing

- Meditating for 5 minutes
- Writing down the next day's schedule

Plan to practice this daily baseline habit(s) for 2 weeks straight. Use a habit tracker or calendar to log your compliance each day.

Part 3: Increase the Challenge

After 2 weeks of consistent practice, it's time for progressive overload - making it harder. Add one of the following:

- Increase the duration or intensity (20 squats instead of 10)
- Stack another small habit (5-minute plank after squats)
- Address a bigger area (decluttering for 15 minutes)

Stick with this new, slightly harder regimen for another 2 weeks. Log in daily.

Part 4: Reward and Reflect

- Give yourself a small reward (a coffee treat, etc.)
- Reflect on how it felt to increase the challenge. Was it hard? Easier than expected?
- Assess any other areas where more discipline would be valuable right now

Part 5: Repeat and Increase

Now that your self-discipline muscle is stronger, repeat the process:

- Keep your baseline habits
- Increase the difficulty again slightly (25 squats, declutter another room, etc.)
- Set a new 2-week goal and track it daily
- Reward, reflect, and increase again

By progressively overloading in this cycle, you'll build mental toughness and lasting self-discipline. The hardest step is sustaining it daily at first, but it gets easier over time.

Reward Systems and Accountability

While self-discipline is an internal force, it can be sustained through external systems like rewards and accountability. These systems not only provide motivation and incentives but also help to reinforce the habits and behaviors that contribute to your success.

Setting Rewards and Consequences

Rewards serve as positive reinforcement, and it provides a sense of satisfaction and enjoyment that reinforces desirable behaviors. Consequences, on the other hand, create a degree of discomfort or negative feedback that discourages undesirable behaviors.

When setting up a reward system, it's important to align the rewards with your personal motivations and values. For some, tangible rewards like treating themselves to a favorite indulgence or activity may be effective. For others, intrinsic rewards like a sense of accomplishment or personal growth may hold greater sway over them.

Regardless of the specific rewards you choose, it's crucial to establish clear, measurable goals or benchmarks that must be met to earn the reward. This allows for a clear connection between the work you put in and the resulting outcome.

Consequences, while potentially less enjoyable, can be equally effective in promoting self-discipline. These might take the form of self-imposed penalties or discomforts, such as donating a sum of money to a cause you don't support, or engaging in an unpleasant task or activity.

As with rewards, it's essential to establish clear guidelines and boundaries around the consequences, ensuring that they are proportionate and reasonable. The goal is not to punish or demoralize yourself but rather to create a gentle nudge that reinforces the importance of adhering to your commitments.

Finding an Accountability Partner

An accountability partner is an individual who has the same objectives as you or understands your journey, and who is willing to hold you accountable to your commitments and progress.

This person can serve as a sounding board, offering objective feedback, encouragement, and constructive criticism when needed. They can also help to celebrate your successes and milestones, reinforce positive behaviors and provide a sense of shared accomplishment.

Ideally, an accountability partner should be someone you trust and respect, someone who is invested in your growth and success. They should be willing to have open and honest conversations, even when those conversations may be challenging or uncomfortable.

In addition to providing accountability, a good partner can also offer a fresh perspective and insights that you may have overlooked. Their objectivity and outside viewpoint can help you to recognize any overlooked blind spots or areas for growth.

It's important to note that the accountability relationship should be a two-way street. Just as your partner holds you accountable, you should be willing to do the same for them, offering support, encouragement, and honest feedback when appropriate.

Tracking Progress and Celebrating Success

When you acknowledge and recognize your achievements, you reinforce the positive behaviors and habits that contribute to your growth, while also providing a much-needed boost to your morale and sense of accomplishment.

There are many methods to monitor your progress, and they range from simple habit trackers or checklists to more sophisticated apps or software tools. The key is to find a method that works for you and one that you'll consistently use and update.

As you track your progress, be sure to celebrate each milestone or achievement, no matter how modest it may seem. These small victories are the building blocks of lasting change and they serve as powerful reminders of your capability and commitment.

Celebrations can vary widely, from indulging in a special activity to simply pausing to reflect on your progress and appreciate your efforts. The act of acknowledging and honoring your successes reinforces the neural pathways associated with those positive behaviors, making it more likely that you'll continue to exhibit them in the future.

Additionally, sharing your progress and victories with your accountability partner, loved ones, or a supportive community can amplify the sense of accomplishment and provide an extra dose of motivation and encouragement.

CHAPTER SIX
Managing Stress And Burnout

We've all experienced stress at some point in our lives, and a certain amount of it can actually be beneficial to keeping us motivated and focused. However, when stress levels become too high and persist for too long, it can have a profoundly negative impact on our productivity and overall well-being.

Elevated stress levels disrupt our thinking, making it difficult to focus, maintain clarity of thought, and reach informed decisions. It saps our energy and motivation, and it leaves us feeling drained and unmotivated to tackle important tasks. Stress also weakens our immune system, which means that we are more susceptible to illnesses that can further derail our productivity.

Subtly, chronic stress can also lead to burnout - a condition of mental, physical, and emotional fatigue stemming from prolonged stress. When we experience burnout, even the thought of work can fill us with dread and our productivity plummets as we lose all motivation. Clearly, effectively managing stress is crucial if we want to maintain high levels of sustainable productivity over the long run.

Understanding the Stress Response

To better manage stress, it's helpful to understand what's happening in our bodies and minds when we experience it. The stress response is a natural biological reaction that occurs when we face a perceived threat or challenge. It initiates the release of hormones such as cortisol and adrenaline, which get our bodies ready to either confront the danger or escape from it.

This survival mechanism served our ancestors well when confronted with life-or-death situations like predatory animals. However, in our modern world, we commonly face psychological and social stressors like work deadlines, interpersonal conflicts, financial pressures, and more. Since our bodies can't distinguish between life-threatening events and everyday stressors, they react the same way physiologically.

When the threat passes, hormone levels are supposed to return to normal. But if the stressor persists day after day, week after week, our bodies remain in a constant state of heightened alertness and arousal. Over time, this persistent triggering of the stress response starts to have an impact, making us vulnerable to various physical and psychological issues.

Recognizing Signs of Burnout

Burnout doesn't happen overnight - it's a gradual process that occurs when we experience high levels of stress for a prolonged period without sufficient recovery time. Being able to recognize the early warning signs can help prevent full-blown burnout from setting in.

Physical Signs:

- Persistent fatigue and exhaustion
- Frequent headaches or muscle tension
- Changes in appetite or sleep habits
- Getting sick more often

Emotional Signs:

- Feeling overwhelmed and unable to cope
- Loss of motivation and energy
- Increased cynicism or detachment
- Sense of dread about going to work

Behavioral Signs:

- Withdrawing from responsibilities

- Increased irritability and impatience
- Procrastination and missed deadlines
- Using food, drugs, or alcohol to cope

If you're experiencing several of these signs, don't ignore them! Burnout only gets worse when left unaddressed. Pay attention to these red flags and take proactive steps to get your stress under control.

The Costs of Chronic Stress

Effectively managing stress isn't just important for productivity - it's essential for our general health and wellness. If chronic stress is not managed, it can result in a range of important health issues, including:

- High blood pressure
- Heart disease
- Obesity
- Diabetes
- Depression and anxiety
- Insomnia
- Digestive issues
- Chronic pain
- Impaired immune function

Additionally, poorly managed stress takes a major toll on our personal and professional lives. At work, it reduces our ability to perform, solve problems, and relate well with colleagues. At home, it strains our relationships with family and friends as we become more irritable, withdrawn, and difficult to be around.

When we're stuck in a cycle of chronic stress, it prevents us from living life to the fullest and being the best versions of ourselves. Taking a proactive approach to stress management allows us to avoid these negative consequences and show up as healthier, happier, higher-performing people in all areas of life.

Stress Management Techniques

Now that we understand the harmful effects chronic stress can have, let's look at some proven stress management techniques you can start implementing right away:

Mindfulness and Meditation

Mindfulness involves intentionally directing your focus to the current moment without passing judgment. It can be developed through meditation, breathwork, or by taking a moment to connect with your senses.

Dozens of studies have demonstrated the stress-reducing benefits of mindfulness. It interrupts the negative thought patterns that perpetuate stress and allows your mind to calm down from its anxious state. Mindfulness gives you greater emotional control and resilience when dealing with stressful situations.

I recommend setting aside at least 5-10 minutes per day to practice mindfulness meditation. There are many free guided meditations available through apps like Calm, Insight Timer, UCLA Mindful, etc. Or you can simply focus on your breathing - inhale for 4 counts, hold for 4 counts, exhale for 6 counts, and repeat.

Don't worry if your mind wanders at first - that's normal! Please gently refocus your awareness on your breath. With regular practice, you'll find it easier to attain a state of focused relaxation.

Exercise and Physical Activity

When you're feeling stressed, getting your body moving is one of the fastest and most effective ways to blow off steam. Exercise provides an outlet for the pent-up energy and tension caused by stress. It also boosts endorphins - the body's natural mood elevators - while reducing hormones like cortisol that contribute to the stress response.

You don't necessarily need to punish yourself at the gym for an hour, though - many studies show that even low to moderate-intensity exercises like walking, swimming, or gentle yoga can significantly reduce stress and anxiety levels. Discovering physical activities that you truly find enjoyable is essential for maintaining consistency with your exercise routine.

I like to keep it simple by going for a brisk 20-30-minute walk outside when I'm feeling overwhelmed. The fresh air, change of scenery, and movement work wonders for clearing my head and regaining my calm focus. Building regular exercise into your routine is an excellent stress prevention strategy as well.

Time Management and Prioritization

A leading cause of stress for many people is feeling like they have too much to do and not enough time. By improving your time management and prioritization skills, you can reduce that overwhelming, out-of-control feeling and work smarter, not harder.

Start by making a list of all your tasks and obligations, then rank them by their true importance. Focus first on accomplishing the highest-leverage activities that will have the biggest positive impact. Be ruthless about eliminating, delegating, or delaying low-priority work where you can.

Next, create a schedule that allocates dedicated time slots for your top priorities. During these blocks, disable your notifications, close your email, and work in a distraction-free environment. You'll be amazed at how much more you can accomplish without constant context-switching.

Work-Life Balance

In our always-on, hustle culture, it's easy to let work take over and consume every waking hour of our lives. But this lack of balance and rest inevitably leads to burnout if we don't establish boundaries.

As important as work is, it can't be the only priority - we need fulfilling personal lives too. Make a point of scheduling quality time with family, friends, hobbies, and pure leisure activities you enjoy. When possible, unplug from work completely during these personal hours.

It's also essential to get sufficient sleep each night. Sleep deprivation undermines our mood, focus, immune function, and overall resilience to stress. Most adults need around 7-9 hours of sleep per night. If you're consistently not getting enough, make getting quality sleep a top priority.

Approach work-life balance with the same dedication you give to work projects. Block off personal time in your calendar. Say no to taking on additional work tasks that would infringe on this time. Draw clear boundaries around when you are and are not available to answer emails or work on certain days.

Setting Boundaries

One key aspect of achieving a better work-life balance is setting healthy boundaries - especially around technology. Our constant connection through smartphones, email, and endless notifications can have us feeling tethered to work 24/7.

To set yourself up for better boundaries, I recommend:

- Disabling email alerts and only checking email during designated work blocks
- Turning off all app notifications except from select people
- Putting your phone on Do Not Disturb mode regularly
- Not checking work messages or email after 7 or 8 pm
- Using website blockers to restrict access to distracting sites during focused work sessions
- Taking real breaks away from screens when possible (e.g. walks, reading an actual book)

It's also important to set boundaries with colleagues, clients, or managers about your availability and responsiveness expectations. Don't be afraid to say something like "I want to give this my full attention, so I may not respond right away in the evenings or on weekends unless it's an emergency." Most rational people will understand and respect that.

Unplugging and Disconnecting

In this age of constant connectivity, hitting the reset button by completely unplugging from technology is one of the most powerful stress relievers available. Taking periodic digital detoxes allows your brain to power down from its usual state of frantic multi-tasking and recharge.

Try designating a time window each week, even if it's just an afternoon or evening, where you turn off all digital devices and commit to being fully present. No phones, laptops, TVs - nothing with a screen. Use this time to read, spend quality time with your loved ones, get out in nature, or simply allow yourself to relax and be bored.

You can even take it a step further by instituting a daily digital curfew or implementing a no-screens rule in certain rooms of your home to create sacred device-free zones. When you're disconnected from the addictive lure and noise of the online world, you may be surprised at how much calmer, recharged, and mentally clear you feel.

You should also aim to completely disconnect for longer periods a few times per year through real vacations and longer breaks. Too many of us remain tethered to work while supposedly "vacationing," which defeats the entire purpose of taking time off to recharge.

Pursuing Hobbies and Interests

Everyone needs activities in their life that spark a sense of enjoyment, creative expression, and meaning apart from their work and responsibilities. Hobbies and interests provide balance, relieve stress, and recharge our motivation and sense of purpose.

What hobby or activity allows you to get into a state of relaxed concentration and creative flow? It could be anything from playing a musical instrument, painting, gardening, woodworking, reading, writing, hiking, or picking up a new skill you've always wanted to learn. The important thing is that it's an outlet that energizes you rather than drains you.

I've found having a couple of go-to calming hobbies like reading fiction and getting outside for long walks makes an enormous difference in my stress levels and overall sense of well-being. Whenever I'm feeling overwhelmed, I know I can shift mental gears by picking up a book or going for a quiet hike in nature to recharge.

Experiment with different hobbies and interests until you find ones that truly allow you to decompress and be present outside of work mode. Build them into your routine as a consistent part of your self-care and work-life balance.

Making Self-Care a Priority

At the end of the day, managing stress comes down to making your overall wellness a true priority rather than just something you aspire to when you "have more time." Well-being isn't a luxury – it's the foundation for sustainable high performance!

Implement a well-rounded self-care practice that incorporates the different physical, mental, emotional, and social needs we all have. Create routines and rituals around activities like:

- Exercise and movement
- Healthy eating habits

- Sufficient sleep & rest
- Unplugging from work & devices
- Pursuing hobbies & interests
- Spending quality time with loved ones
- Relaxation practices like meditation, deep breathing, etc.

Build these self-care practices into your days and weeks just like you would any other important appointment or priority task. Batch them together into designated blocks if needed. If you have trouble sticking with them initially, experiment with techniques like temptation bundling to make them more enticing.

Be proactive about caring for yourself so you can consistently operate at your highest levels of physical energy, mental focus, and personal motivation.

When you've established healthy self-care habits as part of your standard routine, you'll be amazed at how much more resilient you feel in the face of inevitable stressors life throws your way. That inner reserve and balance allow you to maintain your productivity, stay on top of your goals, and ultimately live life more fully.

Taking a comprehensive approach to managing stress, you're investing in your most precious resource - yourself. Make that investment, and you'll see incredible returns in the form of greater health, happiness, and overall life satisfaction.

Temptation Bundling: A Clever Hack to Build Good Habits

Let's face it, we all have guilty pleasures or indulgences that we enjoy, even though we know they might not be the most productive use of our time. Maybe it's watching your favorite Netflix show, scrolling through social media, or indulging in a sugary treat. Whatever your vice, this clever strategy called temptation bundling can help you build good habits while still allowing you to enjoy those little pleasures.

The concept of temptation bundling is simple: you bundle a behavior that you want to encourage like exercising or working on an important project with something you find enjoyable or tempting. By coupling the two activities together, you create a reinforcing pattern that makes it easier to stick to your good habits.

Here's how to implement temptation bundling:

- **Identify your temptation**: What's something you enjoy that you might consider a guilty pleasure or indulgence? It could be watching a certain TV show, listening to a podcast, or eating your favorite snack.
- **Choose a habit to bundle**: Think of a habit or activity you've been wanting to adopt or prioritize, such as exercising, reading, or working on a personal project.
- **Bundle them together**: Only allow yourself to indulge in the tempting activity while you're engaging in the desired habit. For example, you might only let yourself watch your favorite show while on the treadmill or stationary bike, or you can only listen to that addictive podcast while doing meal prep.
- **Be consistent**: Stick to the bundling rule consistently. Over time, your brain will associate the tempting activity with the desired habit, making it easier to stay on track.

The beauty of temptation bundling is that it leverages your existing motivations and desires to build positive habits. Instead of relying solely on willpower or self-denial, you're creating a virtuous cycle where you get to enjoy something you love while also making progress toward your goals.

CHAPTER SEVEN
Mastering Focus And Concentration

In today's fast-moving world, which is full of constant diversions and stimuli vying for our attention, the ability to focus has become an invaluable skill. Whether you're a student striving to excel academically, a professional aiming for career success, or an individual pursuing personal growth, mastering focus and concentration is paramount to unlocking your true potential and achieving your goals daily.

Imagine being able to dive deeply into a task, being able to fully immerse yourself in the present moment, and channel all your mental resources towards a singular objective. This state of deep focus not only enhances your productivity but also allows you to experience a sense of flow, where time seems to stop, and you operate at your peak cognitive capacity. It's a state of being where your best work emerges, and you tap into the depths of your creativity and problem-solving abilities.

The Benefits of Deep Work

In his book "Deep Work," author Cal Newport introduces the concept of deep work, which he defines as "professional activities performed in a state of distraction-free concentration that push your cognitive capabilities to their limit." Engaging in deep work yields numerous benefits, including:

1. **Increased Productivity**: By removing distractions and completely focusing on a task, you can achieve more in a shorter period. Your heightened concentration enables you to work more efficiently and effectively.
2. **Enhanced Cognitive Abilities**: Deep work exercises your brain's capacity for sustained attention, strengthening your

ability to concentrate and think deeply. This cognitive exercise can improve your memory, problem-solving skills, and overall mental acuity.
3. **Higher-Quality Work**: By engaging in deep work, you're able to produce work of a higher caliber. Your undivided attention and intellectual rigor result in more insightful analyses, creative solutions, and innovative ideas.
4. **Increased Job Satisfaction**: Deep work can foster a sense of fulfillment and satisfaction, as you experience the joy of mastering complex challenges and producing meaningful work that leverages your full potential.

Multitasking vs. Single-Tasking

In our quest for productivity, many of us have embraced multitasking as a way to juggle multiple tasks simultaneously. However, research has shown that multitasking can significantly diminish our ability to focus and concentrate effectively.

When we attempt to divide our attention across multiple tasks, our brains are forced to constantly switch between different streams of information and cognitive processes. This context-switching comes at a cost, as our brains are not designed to operate optimally while rapidly shifting between disparate tasks.

In contrast, single-tasking – the practice of focusing on one task at a time – allows us to harness the full power of our cognitive resources and direct them towards a singular objective. By eliminating the need for context-switching, we can achieve a deeper level of concentration and immersion, ultimately leading to increased productivity and better work quality.

The Myth of Multitasking

Despite its perceived benefits, multitasking is often an illusion. While we may feel like we're accomplishing multiple tasks simultaneously, our brains are actually rapidly switching between tasks, which can lead to cognitive overload, decreased performance, and increased stress levels.

Here are some common myths surrounding multitasking:

Myth 1: Multitasking saves time.

Reality: Switching between tasks can actually cost us time and productivity due to the cognitive overhead of context-switching and the increased likelihood of making mistakes or producing lower-quality work.

Myth 2: Some people are better at multitasking than others.

Reality: While some individuals may be more adept at rapidly shifting their attention, research has shown that even those who consider themselves excellent multitaskers still experience cognitive impairments when attempting to juggle multiple tasks simultaneously.

Myth 3: Multitasking is a necessary skill in today's fast-paced world.

Reality: While the ability to prioritize and manage multiple tasks is valuable, attempting to work on several tasks concurrently can be counterproductive. Instead, it's often more effective to practice single-tasking and strategically allocate your time and attention to one task at a time.

By debunking these myths and embracing the power of single-tasking, you can cultivate a deeper level of focus and concentration, ultimately leading to increased productivity, better work quality, and a greater sense of accomplishment.

Improving Concentration

While focus and concentration may come more naturally to some individuals, these skills can be developed and improved through consistent practice and the implementation of effective strategies. Here are some techniques you can incorporate to enhance your ability to concentrate:

Eliminating Distractions

One of the most significant obstacles to maintaining focus is the constant barrage of distractions that surrounds us. From notifications on our devices to environmental noise and interruptions, these distractions can derail our concentration and impede our productivity.

To combat distractions, consider implementing the following strategies:

1. **Minimize Notifications**: Turn off unnecessary notifications on your devices, including email alerts, social media updates, and app notifications that are not essential for your immediate work.
2. **Create a Distraction-Free Environment**: Find a quiet, clutter-free space where you can work undisturbed. Consider using noise-cancelling headphones or instrumental music to block out external noise if needed.
3. **Practice Self-Discipline**: Cultivate the ability to avoid the urge to look at your phone, surf the web, or get involved in other activities. in other distracting activities during focused work sessions.
4. **Use Website Blockers**: Utilize website-blocking apps or browser extensions that can temporarily restrict your accessing distracting websites or social media platforms during specific work periods.
5. **Set Boundaries**: Communicate your focused work times to colleagues, family members, or roommates, and politely ask them to respect your need for uninterrupted concentration during those periods.

The Pomodoro Technique

The Pomodoro Technique is a time management method created by Francesco Cirillo in the late 1980s. This technique leverages the power of focused work intervals and strategic breaks to enhance concentration and productivity.

Here's how it works:

1. **Set a Timer**: Start by setting a timer for 25 minutes, during which you'll work focusing on a particular task without any interruptions or distractions.
2. **Work Uninterrupted**: For the duration of the 25-minute interval, known as a "Pomodoro," fully immerse yourself in the task at hand, resisting the urge to multitask or engage in distracting activities.
3. **Take a Short Break**: Once the Pomodoro is complete, take a short 5-minute break to rest and recharge before starting the next work interval.
4. **Repeat the Cycle**: Repeat this cycle of 25-minute work intervals and 5-minute breaks for as long as needed, taking a longer break (e.g., 15-30 minutes) after every fourth Pomodoro.

The Pomodoro Technique helps you develop the habit of focused work by breaking down tasks into manageable intervals, and it provides structured breaks to prevent mental fatigue and burnout. This technique can be particularly useful for individuals who struggle with procrastination or have difficulty sustaining attention for extended periods.

Brain Exercises and Mindfulness

The way physical workouts strengthen our bodies, participating in mental activities and practicing mindfulness can enhance our cognitive abilities, including focus and concentration. Here are five brain exercises and mindfulness practices you can incorporate into your routine:

1. **Meditation**: Practicing meditation, even for just a few minutes a day, can train your mind to be present and focused. Start by practicing basic breathing techniques or following guided meditation sessions. Over time, you can gradually extend the duration as you grow more at ease with the process.
2. **Mindful Observation**: Engage in mindful observation exercises by focusing your attention on a specific object, sound, or sensation for an extended period. Notice the details, textures, and nuances without allowing your mind to wander.
3. **Memory Games**: Challenge your brain with memory games and exercises, such as memorizing sequences of numbers, words, or images. These activities can improve your working memory and concentration abilities.
4. **Cognitive Puzzles**: Engage in cognitive puzzles, such as sudoku, crosswords, or logic puzzles, to improve your problem-solving skills and boost your capacity to concentrate on intricate tasks.
5. **Mindful Walking**: Practice mindful walking by bringing your full attention to the physical sensations of each step, the rhythm of your breathing, and the sights and sounds around you. This exercise can help cultivate present-moment awareness and improve your overall focus.

Integrating these brain exercises and mindfulness practices into your daily routine can help strengthen your cognitive muscles, making it easier to maintain focus and concentration when tackling demanding tasks or projects.

Optimizing Your Energy Levels

Mastering focus and concentration is not solely about developing mental strategies; it's also crucial to optimize your physical and emotional well-being. When you have abundant energy and a balanced state of mind, you're better equipped to sustain your concentration and perform at your cognitive peak. Just like a high-performance vehicle requires premium fuel and regular maintenance, your body and mind need proper care to function at their best.

Physical Energy Optimization:

1. **Engage in Regular Exercise**: Physical activity is a powerful tool for boosting energy levels. Exercise enhances the flow of blood and oxygen delivery to the brain, releases endorphins that enhance mood, and promotes better sleep quality – all of which contribute to heightened alertness and focus.
2. **Prioritize Nutrition**: What you eat can significantly impact your energy levels. Opt for a balanced diet rich in whole, nutrient-dense foods that provide sustained energy release. Limit processed, sugary foods that can lead to energy crashes. Make sure you drink lots of water throughout the day to stay hydrated.
3. **Practice Good Sleep Hygiene**: Adequate, high-quality sleep is essential for replenishing your energy reserves. Establish a consistent sleep routine, make your sleeping area cozy and avoid drinks with caffeine before bedtime.
4. **Manage Stress**: Chronic stress can deplete your energy and impair your ability to concentrate. Incorporate stress-reducing techniques like deep breathing, meditation, or yoga into your routine.

Emotional Energy Optimization

1. **Cultivate a Positive Mindset**: Your thoughts and emotions can profoundly impact your energy levels. Practice positive self-talk, gratitude, and mindfulness to cultivate a more optimistic and resilient mindset, which can boost your emotional energy.
2. **Find Purpose and Meaning**: Engaging in work or activities that align with your values and provide a sense of purpose can fuel your emotional energy and increase your motivation to stay focused.
3. **Build Supportive Relationships**: Surrounding yourself with a supportive network of family, friends, or colleagues can provide emotional nourishment and encouragement, enhancing your overall well-being and energy levels.
4. **Practice Self-Care**: Engage in activities that bring you happy, relaxed, and refreshed. Whether it's practicing a hobby, spending time in nature, or engaging in creative pursuits, self-care can replenish your emotional reserves.

By optimizing your physical and emotional energy levels, you'll be better equipped to sustain focus and concentration over extended periods. Remember, energy management is an ongoing process that requires self-awareness, discipline, and a commitment to prioritizing your overall well-being. Invest in yourself, and you'll reap the rewards of heightened productivity, enhanced cognitive performance, and a greater sense of accomplishment.

Understanding Circadian Rhythms

Our bodies follow an internal clock called the circadian rhythm. It controls things like when we sleep, release hormones, and process food. Knowing and syncing with your body's internal clock can greatly affect your energy levels and, in turn, your capacity to focus and pay attention.

Each individual has a unique circadian rhythm, with some people being more alert and productive in the morning (known as "larks" or "early birds"), while others thrive during the evening hours ("night owls"). Identifying your personal chronotype, or sleep-wake cycle preference, can assist you in optimizing your daily routine and allocating demanding tasks during your peak productivity periods.

To work in harmony with your circadian rhythm, consider the following strategies:

1. **Establish a Consistent Sleep Schedule**: Try to go to bed and wake up at the same time every day, including weekends, to keep your body's internal clock in check and ensure you get enough sleep.
2. **Leverage Your Peak Performance Times**: Identify your most productive hours and schedule cognitively demanding tasks during these periods when your energy levels and focus are at their highest.
3. **Practice Good Sleep Hygiene**: Create an environment conducive to restful sleep by maintaining a cool, dark, and quiet bedroom, limiting screen time before bed, and establishing a relaxing pre-bedtime routine.
4. **Respect Your Body's Natural Rhythms**: If you're a morning person, prioritize important tasks earlier in the day, while night owls may find it more productive to tackle complex projects in the evening.

By syncing your activities with your body's internal clock, you can boost your energy levels and improve your focus and performance.

Nutrition and Hydration

The foods we consume and our hydration levels can really affect how well we can think, and our ability to focus and concentrate. Eating a balanced diet with lots of important nutrients and staying adequately hydrated can provide the necessary fuel for your brain to operate at its full potential.

Here are some nutritional tips to support optimal focus and concentration:

1. **Eat a Balanced Diet**: Include a range of whole, nutrient-packed foods in your meals, such as fruits, veggies, whole grains, lean meats, and good fats. These foods give your brain the vitamins, minerals, and antioxidants it needs to work well.
2. **Limit Processed and Sugary Foods**: Highly processed and sugar-laden foods can lead to energy crashes and impaired concentration. Instead, opt for complex carbohydrates, which provide sustained energy release.
3. **Stay Hydrated**: Dehydration can negatively impact cognitive performance, including attention, memory, and focus. Try to drink enough water during the day to stay properly hydrated.
4. **Incorporate Brain-Boosting Foods**: Certain foods, such as fatty fish (rich in omega-3s), berries, nuts, seeds, and dark leafy greens, like spinach and kale, have nutrients that help your brain work well and may enhance focus and concentration.
5. **Time Your Meals Strategically**: Avoid consuming heavy or high-fat meals right before mentally demanding tasks, as digestion can divert resources away from cognitive processes. Instead, opt for lighter, nutrient-dense snacks or meals that provide sustained energy.

By fueling your body with the right nutrients and maintaining proper hydration, you can support optimal brain function and improve your ability to concentrate and perform at your best.

Sleep and Rest

Getting enough sleep and rest is really important for keeping your brain working well, including focus and concentration. During sleep, our brains undergo various restorative processes, consolidating memories, replenishing neurotransmitters, and clearing out metabolic waste products that can impair cognitive performance.

Here are some strategies to optimize your sleep and rest for improved focus and concentration:

1. **Prioritize Sleep**: Try to get 7-9 hours of good sleep every night, as recommended by most sleep experts. Consistent, high-quality sleep is crucial for cognitive function, memory, and overall well-being.
2. **Establish a Sleep Routine**: Develop a relaxing bedtime routine, such as taking a warm bath, reading a book, doing some gentle stretching, or practicing meditation. Doing these things can tell your body it's time to relax and get ready for bed.
3. **Create a Sleep-Friendly Environment**: Optimize your sleeping space by keeping it cool, dark, and quiet. Consider using blackout curtains, a white noise machine, or an eye mask to block out potential disturbances.
4. **Practice Good Sleep Hygiene**: Avoid stimulants like caffeine in the afternoon and evening, reduce screen time before bed and do calming activities instead to promote better sleep quality.
5. **Take Strategic Breaks**: During periods of intense focus, take short breaks to allow your mind to rest and recharge. Even brief breaks, such as stretching or taking a short walk, can help reset your attention and improve subsequent focus.
6. **Listen to Your Body**: Pay attention to your body's natural rhythms and fatigue levels. If you're feeling mentally drained or physically tired, it may be time to take a break or prioritize rest to restore your energy and focus.

By prioritizing sleep, establishing a consistent sleep routine, and allowing for strategic breaks and rest periods, you can support your brain's ability to function optimally and maintain sustained focus and concentration throughout the day.

Remember, mastering focus and concentration is not merely a mental exercise; it encompasses a holistic approach that considers your physical, emotional, and environmental well-being.

By following the strategies mentioned in this chapter, you'll be well on your way to unlocking your true potential, boosting your productivity, and achieving your goals daily.

CHAPTER EIGHT
Overcoming Procrastination

In the previous chapters, we've covered a lot of ground when it comes to overcoming laziness and unlocking your true potential. But there's one major obstacle that often gets in the way of making progress - procrastination.

Ah yes, the dreaded p-word. We've all been there - putting off important tasks, delaying what needs to be done, rationalizing why we can do it later. Procrastination is something that plagues everyone from students to CEOs. But the good news is, it's a habit that can be beaten. In this chapter, we're going to dive deep into procrastination - what causes it, why it's so hard to overcome, and practical strategies for finally breaking the cycle.

The Causes of Procrastination

To beat procrastination, we first need to understand what causes it in the first place. Despite what you might think, procrastination isn't just a simple time management issue. There are actually a variety of factors, many rooted in human psychology, that contribute to our tendencies to procrastinate.

- **Fear of Failure**

One of the biggest drivers of procrastination is fear - fear of failure, fear of not being good enough, fear of being judged. When we procrastinate on a task, we're subconsciously protecting our ego from potential failure. It's much easier to continually delay than to try our best and still fall short.

As researcher Nathan DeWall states, "People procrastinate as a way to escape feelings of insecurity surrounding performance abilities...To protect self-worth, people put off the aversive task."

This fear of failure mindset is extremely limiting. It causes us to avoid risks, play it safe, and sell ourselves short of our true capabilities. Overcoming this mental block is crucial for achieving bigger and better things.

- **Impulsiveness**

Another major factor is our struggles with self-regulation and delaying gratification. We're wired to prefer instant gratification over long-term rewards. Checking social media, watching one more episode, taking a longer break - these provide immediate bursts of relief or pleasure. The big goal or important task, on the other hand, requires sustained effort over time.

Behavioral economist George Ainslie found that procrastination is a byproduct of hyperbolically discounting rewards - we disproportionately prefer smaller, sooner rewards over larger, later rewards. It's why we procrastinate and opt for distractions instead of buckling down.

- **Low Task Endurance**

Stanford philosopher John Perry highlights how certain traits, like a "lack of energy" or "lack of self-confidence" can inhibit someone's ability to work on goals and aspirations over a sustained period. Some people simply have a lower threshold for enduring difficult, tedious, or unpleasant tasks before giving in to procrastination.

- **Other Contributing Factors**

There are many other potential factors that enable procrastination, including:

- Poor time management/planning skills
- Underestimating how long tasks will take is known as the Planning Fallacy.
- Task resistance/boredom proneness
- Perfectionism/fear of not doing it perfectly
- Lack of motivation

- Depression/anxiety
- Distractions and temptations in our environment

Often, it's a combination of many of these forces working together that lead us down the procrastination path. Becoming aware of what's really driving this behavior is crucial for addressing it effectively.

The Consequences of Procrastination

Why is overcoming procrastination so important? Because the costs of continually putting things off are incredibly high:

- **Poorer Performance**

Multiple studies have linked procrastination to poorer performance, whether it's lower grades for students or diminished job performance for employees. One meta-analysis found that procrastination is a stronger predictor of lower grades than low IQ.

- **Increased Stress and Health Issues**

The anxiety and guilt from procrastinating, combined with the looming deadlines and time pressure, produce immense stress. Chronic procrastination has been linked to higher rates of insomnia, headaches, digestive issues, colds/flu, and more.

- **Missed Opportunities**

While you're stuck in cycles of delay and inaction, other people are taking initiative and seizing opportunities. Procrastination causes you to miss out on potential life and career opportunities that could move you closer to your biggest goals and dreams.

- **Lower Self-Esteem and Confidence**

Nothing kills self-confidence quite like continually putting things off and breaking commitments to yourself. You start to feel lazy, undisciplined, and like you can't follow through. These narratives soon become self-fulfilling prophecies.

- **Financial Costs**

When you fail to file your taxes on time, miss bill payments, or delay investment indecision it often comes with real financial penalties in the form of late fees, interest charges, and lost potential returns.

- **Relationship Strain**

Procrastinating on chores, errands, or commitments to your partner, family or friends builds resentment and frustration in relationships signals that you don't fully respect others' time and priorities.

Procrastination doesn't just hurt you - it sabotages nearly every area of life. That's why it's absolutely critical to get a handle on this habit.

Strategies to Beat Procrastination

Get Motivated

A key first step is reigniting your motivation for the tasks and goals you're avoiding. Why is this goal important to you? How will achieving it improve your life? What are the consequences of not following through?

- **Visualize the Benefits**

Don't just think about your goals in a detached, abstract way. Vividly visualize what it will feel like to accomplish them - the positive emotions, the increase in confidence and self-respect, and the benefits to your career, relationships, and lifestyle. Make it real in your mind.

As Harvard researcher Richie Davidson states, "We simulate experiences through meditation or visualization...this can fundamentally alter the brain and body."

- **Write Out Your Motivations**

Don't just leave it in your mind. Jot down your motivations on a piece of paper or document you can refer back to. What will achieving this goal mean for you? How will it improve your life?

What are the consequences of not following through? This exercise embeds the reasons more deeply and makes them tangible.

- **Share Your Goals**

Tell close friends and family about the meaningful goals you're working towards. Their encouragement and sense of accountability can provide an added layer of motivation to follow through.

Schedule Your Priorities

One of the best ways to overcome procrastination is by proactively scheduling your priorities and goals into your calendar. Don't leave it up to chance.

Timeboxing

A technique called "timeboxing" involves dedicating set periods of time, usually 1-2 hours, for specific tasks or goals. During this window, you don't allow any distractions or deviation from the task at hand.

Not only does this boost your focus, but inserting immovable blocks into your calendar forces you to make progress rather than continually putting it off. You essentially create a procrastination-free zone for that period.

The 2-Day Rule

Another helpful scheduling strategy is to never leave a task for more than 2 days in a row without making progress on it. If you procrastinated on something yesterday, you have to work on it today, with no exceptions.

This rule, proposed by productivity author James Clear, leverages the power of habit formation. By forcing yourself to revisit the task within 48 hours, you remove the ability for it to lapse entirely

- **Schedule the "Big Rocks" First**

Consider adopting the "big rocks" metaphor when planning your schedule. The big priorities, goals, and obligations are the "big rocks" that should go into your calendar first as immovable blocks. Then you fit the smaller items (meetings, chores, etc) around them.

Too many people make the mistake of scheduling the little things first, leaving no time for their biggest priorities. This inevitably leads to procrastination as the important stuff gets pushed aside. Protect your big rocks.

Remove Distractions

- **Do an Audit**: Start by doing an honest audit of your biggest distractions and temptations at home, work, or wherever you typically procrastinate. Social media? Video games? YouTube binges? Online shopping? TV? Get specific about what sucks you in.
- **Create a Bunker**

Once you identify your kryptonite, it's time to set up a space that helps you concentrate on your work by removing those distractions and temptations. This could mean:

- Deleting time-wasting apps from your phone
- Installing website blockers on your computer
- Leaving your phone in another room
- Relocating to a distraction-free space like a library or coffee shop
- Asking family/roommates to avoid interruptions during certain hours

The goal is to create a procrastination-free "bunker" where you can focus solely on the task at hand without easy temptations in reach. You're making it easier on yourself to stay focused and digging a moat against your procrastination tendencies.

- **Use Incentives**

You can make this removal of distractions more rewarding by combining it with incentives. For example, for every 60-90 minutes of focused, distraction-free work, you can reward yourself with a 15-minute social media break.

Just be careful not to let the "reward" become objective and spiral into procrastination again. Having concrete rules around it can help.

Try Anti-Procrastination Techniques

There are a variety of specific techniques and mind tricks you can use to counteract the urge to procrastinate when it strikes:

The 5 Minute Rule

One highly effective method is to challenge yourself to just get started and work for 5 minutes on the task you're avoiding. That's it, just 5 minutes of focused effort to initiate momentum.

The inertia of being "in" the task, combined with the desire to not have "wasted" those 5 minutes usually propels you to keep going much longer. It's a psychological trick to take advantage of your mindset.

As Gestalt psychology states, "Once a task is initiated, it is easier to terminate it at the end rather than quit in the middle"

The 20-20 Rule

The 20-20 rule was created by personal development author Steve Pavilina, and he recommends working solidly for 20 minutes, then rewarding yourself with a 20-minute break to check emails, grab a snack, etc. Obviously, the time can be adjusted, but the core idea leverages time-boxing and breaks to increase productivity.

Temptation Bundling

This is the idea of only allowing yourself to indulge in guilty pleasures like watching certain shows or listening to podcasts when you're also doing the thing you're procrastinating on, such as exercising. I spoke about this in the previous chapter.

As proposed by Wharton professor Katy Milkman, you "bundle" the want with the should. So maybe you only let yourself listen to that engrossing podcast while you're working on that spreadsheet you've been avoiding. It makes the procrastinated task more enticing.

The key with all these techniques is experimenting to find what works best for your psychological makeup in overcoming procrastination inertia.

Eat That Frog

This classic productivity principle stems from a Mark Twain quote: "Eat a live frog first thing in the morning and nothing worse will happen to you the rest of the day."

In other words, start every day by completing your biggest, most dreaded task before doing anything else. You'll operate from that massive relief and confidence boost for the rest of the day.

Train Your Willpower Like a Muscle

Numerous studies show willpower operates like a muscle that can become depleted through overuse. This partially explains why we tend to procrastinate more later in the day when our reserves are lower.

By consciously "eating the frog" at the start of each day, you're flexing and training your willpower and self-discipline in the most challenging circumstances. Just like how you build physical muscle through strain, this grows your self-regulatory strength over time.

Don't Check Email or Notifications

One massive morning pitfall is getting distracted by emails, notifications, and online activity before you eat the frog. This is a surefire way to get derailed and revert to procrastination.

Instead, keep a proverbial "force field" around you in the morning. Don't check any emails, social media, or notifications until your biggest task is complete. You want to preserve every ounce of morning willpower for conquering the frog.

Leverage Accountability

Humans are "accountability creatures" - we tend to follow through better on goals and tasks when we've made a commitment to others. The mere psychological pressure of accountability can snap us out of procrastination

Get an Accountability Partner

Find a trusted friend, family member, or peer with similar goals and set up an accountability partnership. You can check in with each other regularly on your goal progress, celebrate wins, and encourage each other through rough patches. Consistency is key.

Join a Support Group

In a similar vein, find a group or online community aligned with the goals you're working towards - whether that's a boot camp, workshop, message board, or coaching program. The built-in social support, accountability structures, and shared experiences can be motivating forces.

Ask People to Check In

If you have trouble staying accountable by yourself, be proactive about asking people to check in with you on your progress. For example, your partner, parents, and friends - let them know your targets so they can periodically ask how you're doing.

The mere fact that people are now watching and you've socially committed can be enough to deter procrastination.

Change Your Limiting Beliefs

As we discussed earlier, procrastination is often born from self-limiting beliefs like fears of failure or feeling incapable. These core narratives become self-fulfilling prophecies that reinforce the habit.

Audit Your Inner Monologue

Start paying close attention to the stories and narratives you perpetuate inside your mind about yourself. What do you repeatedly tell yourself about your abilities? Your willpower? Your chances of succeeding?

Write these limiting beliefs down, then interrogate them:

- What evidence is there to support this belief? What contradicts it?
- Where did this belief originate? Is it based on facts or assumptions?
- How has this belief held you back from pursuing goals?
- What would be an alternative, empowering belief to replace it with?

The goal is to shine a light on your negative self-talk and rewrite those scripts into a more productive, capable mindset. This adjustment in your inner monologue is powerful for dismantling procrastination patterns.

Affirmations & Mantras

Another tool is embedding new empowering beliefs through affirmations and mantras you repeat to yourself. For example:

"I'm capable of taking on any challenge I commit to."

"I have incredible self-discipline and follow through on my priorities."

"I'm becoming more focused and productive each day."

Visibility cues like written affirmations, wallpapers, or recordings can reinforce these messages throughout your environment. The key is interrupting the old narratives and instilling new beliefs.

Over time, you start to embody what you've repeatedly affirmed about yourself - including overcoming procrastination during certain times.

Be Patient and Consistent

Like any deeply rooted habit or pattern, overcoming procrastination takes TIME. It's the culmination of diligently applying many of the strategies and techniques covered so far over weeks and months. One breakthrough isn't enough - it requires persistent effort and commitment.

As psychologists Baumeister and Tierney state, "No grand prize is awarded for a single triumph over procrastination. The only way to win is to just keep scoring points, day after day"

So be patient, take it day by day, and trust the long-term process of adjusting your mindset, habits, and environment. Procrastination habits built over many years can't be demolished overnight.

Track Your Progress

You can maintain momentum by tracking streaks of procrastination-free days and periods of high productivity. Marking each successful day on a calendar provides a motivating visual scoreboard. The compounding effect of increased willpower and motivation is incredible.

Just don't let a "slip-up" day completely derail you. Shake it off and get back on track quickly.

Schedule Mental Resets

It's also wise to schedule periodic resets and refocus periods into your routine - whether that's evenings, weekends, quarterly planning sessions, or yearly retreats. Use these as opportunities to:

- Revisit your priorities and reasons for wanting to beat procrastination
- Reflect on recent wins, lessons, and areas for improvement
- Refine and enhance your productivity systems/habits
- Plan and schedule your upcoming sprints

These intentional resets prevent you from aimlessly drifting back into old patterns. Continual realignment is key to making consistent progress.

Additionally, give yourself periodic mental breaks and time completely unplugged to recharge. Pushing too hard for too long often leads to burnout and losing motivation entirely.

Celebrate Milestones

As you accumulate wins and make steady progress towards your anti-procrastination goals, be sure to celebrate the milestones along the way! Completed that big project? Treat yourself to a massage. Crushed your annual targets? Take a vacation.

These "intermittent reinforcements" provide a vital encouragement to stick with the process through the tougher days. They're proof that all your effort is paying off.

Just be careful not to let the celebration bleed back into slippage. Use them as a recharge, then get right back on the horse.

I'll leave you with this - while overcoming procrastination is tough, you absolutely have the capability. Don't let ingrained habits or negative self-beliefs limit what you can achieve.

It starts by believing in yourself and your ability to follow through, then taking it step-by-step. String together a chain of small wins through diligent effort. One by one, you'll dismantle the procrastination patterns and excuses that have held you back.

Eliminating Distractions and Temptations

We live in an age of unprecedented distraction and temptation. Seemingly at every turn, there are rabbit holes to lure us away from our priorities. Overcoming procrastination requires being proactive about removing these destructive forces from your environment.

Perform a Distraction Audit

The first step is to bring awareness to your specific distractions and temptations. These will be highly personal based on your habits and environments.

Some common ones include:

- Social media
- Streaming entertainment (Netflix, YouTube, etc.)
- Online games and apps
- Email/messaging
- Mindless web browsing
- Background TV/radio noise

Make a list of everything that typically derails your focus and productivity. Don't judge yourself - just get it all out on the table.

Remove Digital Temptations

With your list of distractions, now you can start eliminating and controlling your access to them during key work periods.

For digital distractions, this may include:

- Deleting time-wasting apps from your devices
- Installing browser extensions to block distracting websites

- Turning off notifications and alerts
- Implementing temporary internet blockers

You can also explore productivity apps that restrict your access to certain sites/apps except during scheduled break periods.

The goal is to strip away easy avenues for mindless indulgence when you need to concentrate. Addition by subtraction!

Exercise for Mental Clarity

Finally, don't underestimate the mental benefits of physical exercise and movement as an antidote to distractions and procrastination. Exercise physiologist Greg Wells states "Exercise is like a wonder drug for your brain. Rationing exercise is a mistake. People who are sedentary for twelve waking hours a day have a difficult time being focused and productive."

Aerobic exercise improves focus and information processing by increasing blood/oxygen flow to the brain. Resistance training grows and preserves brain tissue. Getting your body moving anchors you in the present moment.

Aim for at least 30-60 minutes of exercise daily, whether that's:

- Going for a walk or run
- Bodyweight exercises or weightlifting
- Yoga or mobility routines
- Playing sports

You can even "bundle" exercise with other tasks like listening to audiobooks or podcasts to multiply the benefits.

Regular physical activity gives you a cognitive edge over the distractions and lack of focus that enable procrastination. Treat exercise as a non-negotiable productivity tool.

Maintain a Distraction Allowed List

Of course, you can't completely eliminate every potential distraction from your life. Certain distractions serve a purpose for breaks, creative inspiration, or simple enjoyment. The key is being intentional about what makes the cut.

Create a short "Distractions Allowed" list of perhaps 2-3 acceptable indulgences like checking social media, watching a show, reading for pleasure, etc. These are your scheduled reprieves and "guilt-free" distractions.

Then, make it a personal policy to ONLY partake in items on that list during specified break periods. No mindless drifting to other sites or apps. This rules-based approach will prevent you from procrastinating further.

You're not aiming for a Spartan, zero-distraction existence. You're just containing distractions to their properly scheduled time-boxes.

Set Productivity Alarms

Another useful strategy is to set recurring alarms or reminders at set intervals (45-60 minutes for example) to check yourself against procrastination.

When the alert goes off, quickly assess:

- Am I working on my highest priority?
- Have I stayed focused and productive?
- Or have I lapsed into distraction/procrastination?

These alarms act like manual circuit breakers to shake you out of autopilot mode. They heighten your self-awareness and accountability in the moment.

With some adjustment, you can make giving into procrastination the harder choice - and productivity the path of least resistance. That's the ideal scenario for achieving your biggest goals!

CHAPTER NINE
Goal Setting And Achievement

In the previous chapter, we did a deep dive into overcoming procrastination - one of the biggest roadblocks to taking action and making progress. Hopefully, you're feeling fired up and equipped with strategies to finally ditch those unproductive habits for good.

Do you know what happens when you consistently take action? You start achieving your goals and ambitions. That's what this chapter is all about - how to set yourself up for goal-crushing success from the start.

We're going to cover everything from the importance of goal setting to different types of goals to pursue, how to formulate an actionable plan, and how to make adjustments along the way. By the end, you'll have a potent blueprint for transforming your goals from wishful thinking into accomplished realities.

The Importance of Goal Setting

Let's start at the very foundation - why is goal setting so vital for growth, productivity, and overall life satisfaction? Working towards goals, both big and small, provides:

- **A Sense of Purpose**

Having clearly defined goals infuses your days, weeks, months, and years with a driving sense of meaning and direction. You're no longer just mindlessly drifting - there's an overarching purpose propelling you forward.

- **Increased Motivation**

Tangible goals are a powerful source of motivation and inspiration. They provide a compelling future vision to strive towards. With each small win along the way, your motivation multiplies.

- **Better Focus and Organization**

Goals structure how we spend our focused brainpower and available time. Studies show that those with goals tend to be less impulsive, more alert to opportunities, and better organized.

- **Higher Achievement**

This one seems obvious, but it's worth stating - decades of research demonstrate that people who set goals achieve far more than those who don't. There's something about the goal-setting process that drives better real-world outcomes.

- **Increased Life Satisfaction**

Ultimately, having goals that excite you, and making progress towards those aspirations, creates far more life satisfaction and positive feelings than just going through life aimlessly

Goals provide the substance that allows us to live up to our fullest potential as humans. They push us to grow, contribute, and leave an impact on the world.

The Benefits of Goal Setting

Before we break down tactics and strategies, it's worth highlighting some of the psychological benefits you can expect from effective goal setting:

- **Clarity and Vision**

Good goals plainly describe where you want to go and what you need to achieve. They transform our fuzzy desires into clear, vivid visions that are easier to plan for and execute.

- **Accountability**

When you lay down tangible goals you can hold yourself accountable to hitting those marks. Goals become personal yardsticks for judging your progress and results, thus increasing your personal responsibility.

- **Prioritization**

Goals force you to look at your life, responsibilities, and ambitions through an impartial lens. With clear goals, you can better prioritize what really matters rather than waste time.

- **Reduced Overwhelm**

Have you ever felt paralyzed by all the different tasks and responsibilities on your plate? Goal setting helps alleviate that overwhelming feeling by helping you whittle down your focus to key objectives.

- **Personal Growth**

The very act of pursuing goals that push you out of your comfort zone catalyzes the start of a personal evolution. You naturally cultivate new skills, knowledge, habits, and mindsets along the way.

- **Increased Confidence**

As you start achieving goals and collecting "wins", big and small, your self-confidence increases. Success breeds more success through positive reinforcement cycles.

Types of Goals to Pursue

The first step to setting goals is to determine WHAT goals you actually want to set and pursue in your life. These will vary based on your personal priorities, circumstances, and what stage of life you're in.

Generally, there are a few common categories that effective goals tend to fall under:

- **Career or Professional Goals**

What milestones do you want to reach in your professional journey? Getting a promotion or raise? Launching a business? Finding your dream job? Getting additional certifications or education? Define the rungs on your career ladder.

- **Financial Goals**

Many people crave the freedom and security that comes with financial stability and wealth. Popular goals in this bucket include:

> - Getting out of debt
> - Buying a home
> - Saving for retirement
> - Growing investment accounts
> - Reaching certain income or net worth levels
> - Health & Wellness Goals

Given the central importance of our physical and mental health, some examples are Weight loss, building strength/endurance, eating a balanced diet, cutting unhealthy habits, sleeping better, reducing stress, etc.

- **Skill Development**

What new skills, knowledge, or abilities do you want to build? Learning an instrument, coding, a second language, public speaking, or anything that allows you to grow and increase your capabilities.

- **Experiential**

Don't neglect goals around doing and experiencing as well. Things like:

> - Travel to certain destinations
> - Starting a bucket list and working through it
> - Spending more quality time with loved ones
> - Participating in events like marathons or competitions

Contribution or Impact

Many find great fulfillment in goals oriented around making a positive impact beyond themselves. This could be volunteering, donating money or resources to causes, starting a non-profit, mentoring others, activism, etc.

Within these categories, you'll want to mix shorter-term goals that can be achieved soon with longer-range ambitions that will take more consistent effort over time.

And of course, these suggestions are just a framework - your specific goals should align with your personal values, interests, and vision for your life's journey.

Aligning Goals with Personal Values

For goals to be highly motivating and meaningful, it's critical that they sync up with your personal values and life vision. If not, you'll inevitably feel disconnected from the goals and struggle to sustain motivation over time.

Exercise

One exercise for identifying your value-aligned goals is to write out a list of your values - the guiding principles that are most important and meaningful to you. Examples could include:

- Family and Relationships
- Personal Growth
- Financial Security
- Adventure or Freedom
- Creativity or Self-Expression
- Spirituality
- Community
- Achievement or Success
- Philanthropy or Giving Back

Once you have this values list, go through each one and explicitly state 1-2 goals you could set that would allow you to live more in accordance with that value.

So for "Family and Relationships" you might put "Schedule a monthly date night and family weekend activity" to reinforce the importance of quality time.

For "Personal Growth" maybe it's "Read 1 book per month on a topic of interest" so you're feeding your growth mindset.

And so on, linking each of your personal values to concrete goals that honor those values.

- **Visualize Your Ideal Future**

Another perspective to consider is imagining your ideal vision for the coming years of your life. What does your "perfect day" look like? Where are you living, who are you surrounded by, and what fulfill you?

Don't censor or judge these visions - allow yourself to dream in vivid detail. Then analyze - what tangible goals would need to be achieved in order to manifest that ideal future.

The goals need to inspire you toward your biggest hopes, dreams, and sources of meaning. That's when you'll be able to summon and sustain your motivation easily.

Creating an Action Plan

At this point, you have some goals set that are motivating, meaningful, and match up with your life's vision and values. Now it's time to get ultra-specific with the HOW - your action plan for making these goals a reality.

Going in with a solid action plan exponentially increases your chances of achieving success. As they say, "A goal without a plan is just a wish."

The most effective plans contain these key elements:

- **Clearly Defined Goals**

Your actual goals need to be clear, specific, and unambiguous. "Getting healthier" is vague, but "losing 15 lbs" is straightforward. "Being more productive" is not as clear as "Waking up at 6 am daily."

Write down the precise goals in affirmative statements and avoid vague language. This makes them concrete and easier to plan for.

- **Measurement & Milestones**

Specify how you will measure or assess progress for each objective. This could be metrics like:

> - Weight or body measurements for fitness goals
> - Income or net worth numbers for financial goals
> - Test scores or completed projects for education goals
> - Books read or languages learned for skill goals

Then set incremental milestones to hit along the way. Milestones provide psychological wins that sustain motivation.

- **Start & End Dates**

Each goal should have a clearly designated start date for when you'll kick things off, as well as a specific end date for when you want to have it achieved.

The end dates create urgency and eliminate open-endedness. Just be realistic when setting them.

- **Required Actions**

Perhaps the most important is that you need to map out all of the specific actions, behaviors, and tasks required to reach your end goal and hit those milestones. Don't assume you'll figure it out as you go.

For example, if your goal is to launch a business, some required actions could include:

- Validating product or market fit
- Forming a legal entity
- Creating a website or branding
- Finding suppliers or contractors
- Building an initial customer base

Leave nothing to chance! The more comprehensive your required actions list, the clearer the path forward.

Potential Obstacles

It's also wise to proactively identify any potential obstacles, risks, or challenges that could get in the way of executing your goal plan. Things like:

- Lack of money or funding
- Needing to learn key skills
- Personal limiting beliefs or fears
- Finding time alongside other commitments
- Getting buy-in from others involved

With these listed, you can start to plan for how you'll mitigate, work around, or eliminate those roadblocks from stunting your progress.

Support Needed

Another element to consider is what resources, tools, or support from others you'll need access to in order to achieve the goal. This could include:

- Hiring assistance like coaches, consultants, agencies
- Purchasing software, equipment, or materials
- Finding an accountability partner
- Getting backing from your family or employer

Identify these in advance so you can start lining up what's needed from the beginning.

Essentially, you want to make your action plan so thorough and comprehensive that you can't realistically make excuses for not following through. It eliminates ambiguity and replaces it with clarity around your required tasks and schedule.

The simple act of committing this level of forethought to a written plan drastically improves your chances of making it happen. That's a motivating feeling in itself!

Breaking It Down Into Actionable Steps

Translating your most ambitious goals into clearly defined, actionable steps that feel manageable and non-overwhelming is crucial for maintaining motivation and working steadily over longer periods of time. When something feels too lofty or insurmountable, it's easy to procrastinate or avoid it. Bite-sized steps keep you moving.

Use the "Backward Planning" Approach

A helpful technique is to start with your goal's big endpoint and work backwards to reverse-engineer all the steps required at each stage.

For example, if your goal is to write and publish a book within 12 months:

1. The ultimate step is hitting "publish"
2. Before that, you need a final edited manuscript
3. Before that, you need a complete first draft
4. Before that, you need an outline and writing schedule
5. Before that, you need book concept ideas
6. And so on, all the way back to step 1

By breaking it down this way, you create a roadmap of clearly identified tasks leading up to your goal. No more overwhelming uncertainty around "How do I even start?"

This approach works for professional goals (e.g. getting a promotion), financial goals (e.g. saving for a home downpayment), or any other goal you're pursuing.

Use a PERT Chart

For highly complex goals with numerous dependencies and moving parts, you may want to employ a PERT chart program - Program Evaluation Review Technique.

This visual tool maps out all tasks in a logic sequence, including:

- Task names and detailed descriptions
- Durations for each task
- Dependencies on other tasks
- Start and end dates
- "Milestones" indicating key accomplishments

PERT charts provide a comprehensive roadmap for managing intricate, multi-step goals and initiatives where things need to happen in a specific order.

Identify Low-Hanging Fruit

Once you have your goal broken down into actionable tasks, do a pass to identify any "low-hanging fruit" - easy wins you can quickly knock out to build some momentum early on.

For example, if you're launching a new business, maybe some of the low-hanging fruit tasks are:

- Setting up your website domain/hosting
- Incorporating your business with the state
- Ordering basic marketing materials
- Finding your first few customers or clients

Don't overlook or underestimate these small progress tasks! Each one you check off is a minor victory that builds positive reinforcement towards the bigger goal.

Setting Deadlines and Milestones

Deadlines are psychological motivators. Something about a harsh deadline lights a fire under us and creates an urgency to execute.

However, your deadlines should strike a balance. If your goal's end deadline is too far out into the future, it can actually have a. Opposite motivating effect. Your mindset becomes "Eh, I still have plenty of time..." and procrastination sets in.

That's why it's important to set periodic milestone target deadlines every few weeks or months to build in urgency and accountability. These deadlines create psychological tension and pressure to keep progressing.

Missing your deadlines is also valuable data! They cue you to re-evaluate aspects of your plan - were the deadlines wholly unrealistic? Does your execution need to get tighter? Where are the friction points?

The Risk or Reward Element

Adding an extra layer of stakes and psychology around your goals can amp up motivation even more. Some ways to do this are:

Set Rewards for Hitting Milestones

Outline meaningful "prize" rewards for yourself when you hit certain milestones or the final deadline.

Have Accountability "Punishments"

Similarly, you can set accountability punishments if you miss milestone or final deadlines. These could be foregoing certain indulgences, paying a cash penalty to someone, or other deterrents that up the personal stakes.

Make Physical Bets or Challenges

Take it a step further by making your goal a quantifiable physical challenge or bet - for example, running a half marathon in a certain time, doing 1,000 pushups before a set date, or hitting a revenue target to avoid a punishment like shaving your head.

The more real and tangible the rewards/punishments linked to your goals, the more motivating they become. Just be careful not to make the stakes so extreme that you feel stuck!

Tracking and Evaluating Progress

Tracking and evaluating your progress along the way helps you to keep consistent data inputs to evaluate if you're on track (or falling behind), then make informed adjustments or change your approach as needed.

Without frequent progress tracking and evaluation cycles, you could accidentally go months or years in the wrong direction before realizing you're hopelessly off-course from your original goal.

Use a Goal Tracking System

The simplest way to stay on top of your progress is to implement a dedicated goal-tracking system or routine. This could be a digital tool like a spreadsheet, an app or software. Or it could be an analog approach like a physical journal, planner or vision board.

Conduct Weekly Reviews

Beyond the daily app tracking, set a recurring weekly review session - ideally on the same day or time each week when you can go a little deeper. In these sessions, you'll analyze:

- Which tasks, habits or actions drove you closer to your goals?
- What setbacks or roadblocks did you face? How can you adjust?
- Are you currently making adequate progress toward upcoming milestones?
- Where did you get off-track or procrastinate? Get honest!

These focused weekly reviews allow you to evaluate what's working (or not) while the previous week is still fresh. Adjust your plan and approach accordingly for the upcoming week.

Monitoring and Adjusting Goals

Once you've diligently tracked your goal progress and you notice some warning signs and speed bumps, you'll need to adjust your plans and approaches according to your current realities.

It's like driving toward a destination. You started out with certain directions, but sometimes some roadblocks, detours, and changing conditions will inevitably require you to adjust your route and driving approach along the way.

Euphio Question Technique

One advanced methodology is the "Euphio question technique" which has you repeatedly asking specific questions about your goal and progress:

Euphio = the Greek words Eu "good" and Phio "I bear" - to yield good.

The process involves regularly asking yourself 3 cyclical questions:

Q1:   Is this goal and plan realistically possible given my current realities/situation?

- If not, you may need to overhaul the goal itself or massive aspects of the plan

Q2:   Will this goal or plan yield good results by following it?

- Is forward progress happening as expected? If not, you likely need to course-correct

Q3:   What's the highest point of leverage to improve the existing plan?

- Identify any bottlenecks or friction points to fix based on learnings so far

By intentionally exploring these angles, you're staying proactive about aligning your goal pursuits with rapidly changing realities on the ground.

In instances where you're clearly falling short of the milestones and deadlines in your goal plan based on incoming data, you have a few options:

Take a Step Back

The potentially harsh reality is that the goal may have been too big, the deadlines too aggressive, or your current situation is prohibitive to success. Retreat and reassess with a clear mind:

- Do you need to extend certain milestone dates to ease the pressure?
- Should you scale the goal itself back to be more realistic initially?
- Is this even the right goal to be pursuing right now given the constraints?

Get out of any precipice mindset and embrace flexibility here. Temporary stagnation is better than costly failure.

Boost Commitment and Effort

If the goal realignment seems relatively feasible with some tweaks, perhaps the core issue is your level of commitment and effort output.

- Are you skipping steps or cutting corners in your execution?
- Have you let motivation and urgency wane without accountability?
- Are you not deploying maximum effort consistently?

In these cases, stepping up your commitment and effort levels may be all that's needed to get back on track towards the goal.

Change Your Approach

Sometimes the goal itself is still valid and motivating, but your specific approach and plan just aren't yielding the desired results. This calls for you to try a new methodology or path.

- Does your current plan have too many dependencies causing bottlenecks?
- Could a different tactic, technique or philosophy work better?
- Are there modern tools or technologies you're not leveraging?

No Regrets: Abort Mission

There's also the chance that as new data surfaces, you realize a particular goal just isn't as meaningful or worth the investment as you initially thought. Your priorities can shift over time.

If that's the case, permit yourself to abort the mission entirely, with no regrets. Failed goals can provide valuable lessons, but there's no nobility in endlessly persisting down a path you've lost passion for.

Take out the learnings, update your priorities, and reallocate your efforts in a more fruitful direction. Goals are great, but don't let them send you into an existential crisis.

The key is monitoring your journey consistently and objectively, and then making difficult decisions when adjustments are required. Don't get so attached to the original plan that you ignore reality.

The goals and dreams that truly matter are well worth the complexities and shifts needed to see them through!

CHAPTER TEN
Maintaining Momentum And Consistency

You learned how to set meaningful goals aligned with your values and vision, create comprehensive action plans, track progress, and make adjustments along the way.

But now we need to talk about what may be the most difficult part of any personal growth journey - maintaining consistent momentum over longer periods of time. It's one thing to set audacious goals and sprint out of the gates for a few weeks or months. It's an entirely different challenge to grind it out day after day, week after week, year after year.

That's what separates those who achieve incredible long-term success from those who fizzle out and revert to old habits and patterns.

The Importance of Consistency

Before we get into specific tactics, let's talk about why striving for consistency is so vital when pursuing big goals and ambitions:

- **Compound Interest Towards Your Vision**

The powerful concept of compound interest doesn't just apply to wealth-building - it governs progress in nearly any endeavor. Small, consistent steps and wins build upon themselves exponentially over time.

For example, if you only write 500 words per day towards your book goal, that's over 180,000 words in a year - more than enough for most books. But if you only write sporadically whenever motivation strikes, you'd be lucky to finish a single chapter annually.

- **Sustainable is the New Extreme**

In a society that loves hacks and life-changing events, it's easy to get seduced by unsustainable "extreme" paths and challenges. While doing something drastic for a finite period can create an exciting transformation, very few people can maintain that level of intensity permanently.

Consistency, on the other hand, represents a more realistic and sustainable approach to achieving incredible results over the long haul.

- **Habit Formation**

The activities and behaviors required for any major goal can only become a habit through repetition and consistency over time. It's been shown that habits take a minimum of 60-90 days to really solidify in your psyche and daily routines.

- **Own Your Identity**

Those who achieve and maintain consistency start to take on the qualities of their goals as part of their identity. This transition from aspiring to embodying is incredibly empowering. You begin to own the identity of "I am someone who does X daily."

The opposite also holds true - those lacking consistency confuse their identity and send unconscious de-motivating signals of "I'm not really about this after all." Taking massive action consistently is how you live into your grandest visions.

- **Overcoming Setbacks and Obstacles**

Of course, no path towards an ambitious goal is perfectly linear. Life inevitably throws curve balls our way in the form of setbacks, obstacles, failures, motivational slumps, and other frustrating detours.

The difference between those who ultimately achieve their goals and those who abandon the pursuit often comes down to their reactions and mindset towards adversity. It's not about avoiding setbacks entirely - it's about developing resilient systems and strategies for persisting through them.

Here are some approaches to employ when those challenging chapters arise:

- **Reframe "Failure" as Data**

One of the most empowering mindset shifts you can make is reframing any perceived "failures" as simply insightful data points on your path of progress. Every time something doesn't go as planned, you have the opportunity to:

> ➢ Analyze objectively what went wrong and why
> ➢ Extract valuable lessons and learnings for future iterations
> ➢ Adjust your approach based on real-world feedback
> ➢ Build more robust systems to compensate for weaknesses

With this reframe, even massive "failures" are simply providing the raw intelligence necessary to iterate more intelligently towards your ultimate vision and goals. Every setback is truly just a setup for an even bigger eventual comeback.

- **Implement "Failure Protocols"**

To take this principle even further, it can be valuable to proactively outline "failure protocols" for the most likely setbacks related to your specific goals. How will you respond when X happens? What are your contingencies to get back on track?

For example, if you're pursuing fitness goals, your failure protocols could be outlined:

> ➢ Injury response plans for rehab and recovery
> ➢ Contingencies for sickness or obligations knocking you off track

- ➢ Specific steps for regaining consistency after motivation dips
- ➢ Strategies for adjusting workouts if plateaus hit

Having these pre-meditated recovery systems at the ready can minimize the delays and damage control required when adversity arises. You're able to stay solution-oriented.

- **Use Accountability for Resilience**

Setbacks become exponentially more difficult to navigate when you don't have a supportive environment holding you accountable. This is why having the right group, partners or mentors in your corner proves invaluable.

They can step in during moments of doubt or failure to:

- ➢ Empathize and remind you failure is natural and temporary
- ➢ Reinforce a positive long-term mindset about your capabilities
- ➢ Share their own stories of resilience to inspire perseverance
- ➢ Realign yourself with your deeper "Why" motivations
- ➢ Ask productive questions to reframe the setback
- ➢ Hold you accountable to getting back on track swiftly

In short, the right accountability network can be the difference between you taking a small detour and completely derailing from the track.

- **Meditate and Refocus**

Mental resilience plays a huge role in productively working through adversity as well. Practices like meditation, mindfulness, and breathwork can strengthen this "muscle" tremendously.

You're more able to calmly process the situation and take positive steps forward. Additionally, using meditative techniques to realign with the deeper "Why" behind your pursuits can be powerfully reinvigorating. Sometimes getting bogged down by the day-to-day setbacks we face causes us to lose sight of our biggest inspirations for growth.

The Compound Effect

In case you're not familiar, the compound effect is the principle of small efforts, habits or accomplishments accumulated consistently over time resulting in massively disproportionate outcomes and progress.

It's inspired by the concept of compound interest, where relatively small contributions add up exponentially year over year when growth is allowed to compound upon itself continually.

This concept flies in the face of our cultural fixation with having monumental breakthroughs or achieving overnight success. However, the research conclusively shows that the strategy of making small, sustainable improvements on a consistent basis generates far greater and longer-lasting results.

Let me walk through a couple of examples to make this tangible for you and your goals:

Writing a Book with the Compound Effect

Let's say your goal is to write a 250-page book. Initially, that probably sounds incredibly daunting and like a ton of effort, right? But what if you approached it this way:

- Commit to writing just 500 words per day, every day. (That's about 2 pages)
- That's only an hour or two of dedicated "butt in chair" time
- After one year, you'd have over 180,000 words - enough for a full book PLUS a decent head start on your next one! All

from just sticking to a very manageable consistent daily word count.

It's a far cry from the overwhelming mental image of banging out a whole book in a short time. The compound effect allows you to take small consistent steps that inevitably build the momentum to reach that seemingly monumental goal.

Developing Expertise

Psychologists have found that it takes most people to require more than 10,000 hours of focused practice to achieve mastery of a skill.

That may sound overwhelming, but it averages out to just:

- 5 hours per week for 40 years
- 10 hours per week for 20 years
- 20 hours per week for 10 years

Again, the road to mastery is much more palatable and achievable when you commit to consistent, sustainable practice over long periods rather than unrealistic intensity. Small but persistent incremental gains are what build elite performance.

Staying Motivated and Inspired

We all inevitably experience cyclical dips in motivation, inspiration, and general enthusiasm when pursuing our biggest goals.

Those are the periods that can derail your incredible progress and send you off the rails and back into old patterns and habits if you leave them unaddressed. It's human nature to struggle with sustaining effortful behaviors long-term without occasional breaks or renewal.

This is why having reliable strategies and systems for actively managing your motivation and inspiration levels is so crucial for maintaining momentum over time.

Here are some of the most powerful approaches I've found for staying constantly inspired, motivated, and "stoked" about living to your highest vision and potential:

- **Revisit and Evolve Your Whys**

Your deepest motivations for personal growth and goal achievement need to have profound meaning and significance to you. They can't just be surface-level aspirations without roots.

That's why it's so valuable to periodically revisit and even re-evaluate the "Whys" behind the specific outcomes you're pursuing. Going through this exercise reinforces both the intellectual and emotional drivers that provide purpose.

For example, your surface-level goal may be to get physically fit and healthy. But what are the reasons behind that basic outcome? To:

- Be an energetic, present parent able to play with your kids
- Have the confidence and stamina to adventure
- Reduce the chances of chronic illnesses as you age
- Feel attractive and self-assured in your body
- Be a positive example of discipline for those around you

The more vividly you can articulate and connect with your reasons at an emotional, and psychological level beyond just the basic goal - the more renewable your motivational fuel becomes.

You're reminding yourself why this difficult path matters beyond just checking boxes.

- **Leverage Peak Experiences**

We all have vivid memories of awe-inspiring "peak moments" that filled us with motivation, aliveness, and belief in our highest possibilities - whether that was:

- A mind-blowing travel adventure

- An intense workout or athletic achievement
- An epic creative release like writing, performing, etc.
- Witnessing the birth of a child or other profound life event
- A mind-expanding book, workshop, or learning experience

Rather than letting those peaks fade into memory, you can actively practice re-immersing yourself in the mental or emotional states they produced like:

- Creating a "peak experience" vision board or collection
- Writing vividly detailed journal accounts to remember everything
- Recording videos that can transport you back into the experience
- Building routines that emulate the physical or mental feelings

- **Surround Yourself with Elevators**

Your immediate environments and social circles undoubtedly play a massive role in the motivational energy available to you on a daily basis. It's human nature to absorb the mindsets and attitudes of those you spend the most time around.

With that in mind, be extremely selective about who and what you're allowing into your personal air space. Toxic negativity, fixed mindsets, and scarcity mentalities are a form of motivational kryptonite that will slowly drain your drive.

Instead, make it a priority to intentionally surround yourself with "Elevator" people and influences - those who exude the motivations, disciplines, and success-oriented mindsets you're aspiring towards. They should consistently elevate your energy and inspiration levels just by being present.

This could mean:

- Joining transformational communities of inspiring peers

- ➢ Investing in coaches or mentors who exude the right mindsets
- ➢ Reading biographies/works of visionaries in your field
- ➢ Consuming content from motivational speakers/leaders
- ➢ Being selective about social gatherings, even with family
- **Build Motivation Rituals**

You can hard-code motivational patterns into your daily routines. The most powerful mindsets and behaviors ultimately turn into unconscious habits.

Some examples of potential motivation rituals:

- ➢ Listening to motivational audio while exercising
- ➢ Keeping artifacts or visual cues related to your "Whys" around your physical space
- ➢ Scheduling recurring mindset coaching or breathwork

Celebrate Your Damned Wins!

In the relentless pursuit of your ambitious goals, it's easy for you to move on to the next target without appreciating how far you've already come. This is a surefire way to burn out motivation over time.

Make it a consistent habit to pause and actively celebrate each meaningful milestone, accomplishment, or evolution you achieve along the way. Ideally, you'll want to both:

1. Internally acknowledge, embrace, and FEEL the emotional satisfaction and growth from the experience to solidify confidence.
2. Find a way to tangibly treat yourself and loved ones through rewards like:
- Dinner celebrations
- Experiences like trips or entertainment
- Small indulgences or gifts

- Throwing a party!

Don't brush off these little victories as no big deal. Let yourself FULLY enjoy these wins before moving on to the next mountain to climb. You deserve to feel proud of the immense effort personal growth requires!

CONCLUSION
Embracing A Productive And Fulfilling Life

What an incredible journey we've been on together! We've covered so much ground - from digging deep into the root causes of laziness and its impacts, all the way to developing productive mindsets, mastering skills like goal-setting and time management, and learning how to sustain motivation for the long haul. Seriously, kudos to you for sticking with it!

If you've absorbed even a little bit of the wisdom packed in this book, I'm confident your productivity, goal achievement, and overall life satisfaction are about to level up in ways you can't even imagine yet. It's going to be a total game-changer.

But before we wrap things up, we need to revisit the biggest underlying message here - one that goes beyond all the specific tactics and strategies I've discussed. This personal growth path you've committed to isn't just about checking off more tasks or crushing goals (although that's definitely an awesome side effect!).

The deeper opportunity is about fundamentally upgrading your entire life experience by becoming a productive, purposeful, and growth-oriented person.

Choosing to cultivate productivity at this foundational level is a value statement. It's you telling yourself and the universe: "I deeply care about my growth and contributions." "I'm going to be intentional with how I use my limited time and energy." "I deserve to feel that pride of accomplishment." "I'm committed to doing the work to create a positive impact, big or small."

If that resonates with you, then embracing productivity isn't a sacrifice at all. It's choosing to fully inhabit and optimize this one life you've been given. And it's an incredibly profound gift you can give yourself!

The Human Potential Is Limitless

I want you to know that you can literally keep learning and getting better at things FOREVER. Your minds and talents have no actual limits or ceilings! Can you believe that? No matter how smart or skilled you become, there will always be new frontiers and possibilities to explore next. The growth and discovery never have to stop!

But here's the catch - the only true boundaries are the ones you create yourselves by having negative, limiting thoughts. Like if you tell yourself "I'm not good at that" or "I'll never be able to do that."

So the key is to approach this amazing lifelong journey of growth with an open, curious, and humble mindset. Stay endlessly interested in stretching your skills, experiences and abilities higher and higher. Never be satisfied with how good you are right now.

I can absolutely guarantee you this: if you nurture that burning hunger to keep evolving, then every new accomplishment - every new mountain you climb - will open up entirely new and mind-blowing vistas of human potential that you never could have even conceived of beforehand! It will literally blow your mind over and over again. The possibilities are endless when you just embrace a growth mindset.

If you can remain truly steadfast in your commitment to continually expand your capacities like that, then each chapter of your life will exponentially raise the bar for what's possible in the next. Meaning, you'll achieve something that blows your mind. But then, that will just become the new baseline for an even crazier, more awesome dream to manifest next! It's like climbing an endless staircase into your greater and greater potential.

The real reward here isn't just achieving tasks and goals, though that's great too. No, the deeper prize is developing an intense zeal, curiosity, sense of purpose and adventure in life itself. Where every new day feels like a gift to unwrap and fully participate in.

By fully committing to conscious productivity, you're firmly planting yourselves in the driver's seat of your destinies. You're taking radical responsibility for authoring the stories being written on the canvases of your existence.

And let me tell you, that is an awesome power that relatively few humans throughout history have been intentional and disciplined enough to actually wield consistently. Just look around at the dullness, stagnation and mediocre results surrounding us - that's proof of how rarely this wisdom gets embodied.

So as you progress on these personal journeys of growth, I really want to encourage you to find fulfillment in the journey itself, not just obsessing over specific accomplishments or endpoints. Of course, definitely celebrate with huge excited energy when you achieve those big milestones! You absolutely should.

It's about rediscovering the pure joys, freedoms, and feelings of creative empowerment that come from:

- Being in full command of how you spend your time, energy and life priorities
- Actively shedding old comfort zones to continually embrace new learning edges
- Living with the awareness that you're having a positive impact on those around you
- Surprising yourselves by demolishing self-limiting doubts and rising into greater self-beliefs
- Finally feeling like you're answering your most authentic callings that laziness once muffled
- Building an unshakable confidence by boldly leaning into your full potential

The Journey Is the Real Reward

As I'm sure you can tell, this entire process has been an invitation to view productivity as way more than just dry tactics for checking things off your to-do list. I've really aimed to reframe it as a treasured life philosophy - an avenue to profoundly elevate your overall human experience.

Yes, consistently applying productivity principles will absolutely help you accomplish far more tasks, goals and ambitions.

But the deeper "wealth" you'll accrue is an intrinsically motivated zest for life, a contagious spirit of curiosity, purpose and adventure that makes each new day feel like a gift to unwrap and fully participate in.

By committing to conscious productivity, you're firmly planting yourself in the driver's seat of your destiny. You're taking radical responsibility for authoring the story written on the canvas of your existence.

That's an awesome power that relatively few humans have been intentional enough to wield throughout history. Just look around at the mediocre results - it's proof of how scarce this wisdom remains.

So as you progress on this journey, I encourage you to find fulfillment in the journey itself, not just obsessing over discrete accomplishments. Definitely celebrate when you hit those huge milestones when they come! But more importantly, learn to appreciate the simple act of spending your days optimized and progressing in harmony with your deepest values and visions.

That's the true essence of a life well-lived through productive principles. It's about rediscovering the pure joys and freedoms of:

- Being in command of your time, energy and priorities
- Shedding stagnant comfort zones to continually embrace your edges
- Having a positive impact on those around you

- Surprising yourself by demolishing self-imposed limitations
- Finally answering those authentic callings that laziness muffled
- Building unstoppable confidence by boldly leaning into your potential

So wherever this personal journey ultimately leads you, whatever ambitions you decide to pour yourself into, keep coming back to that foundational context of why this work matters so deeply.

Yes, because you'll get to enjoy the tangible fruits of your efforts - the income, possessions, status or whatever external rewards motivate you temporarily.

Contributing Your Verse

As this book comes to an end and you embark on integrating these teachings, let me leave you with one final metaphor for why investing in productivity is so vital:

Life is like a big play happening on a stage. Some people are the actors, some help make the scenery and costumes, and some just watch.

The whole universe is the biggest stage of all, with many smaller stages within it for all the different worlds and stories happening.

Our world, planet Earth, is one of those big stages. For thousands of years, billions of people have played different roles in the big play happening here - as actors, helpers, or audience members watching the story unfold.

Each person's life is like a small scene or verse in this giant play. You get to be on stage for a little while before others take your place.

When it's your turn on stage, you have an important choice. Will you just say your lines and do what you're told, without really putting in any effort? Or will you practice really hard, give it your full energy and passion, and add your own creative twist to your scene to make it better?

The people who really focus, work hard, and put their whole heart into their scene are the true stars. Through their dedication, they make the whole play more amazing. They inspire the other actors and add totally new ideas that take the story in fantastic new directions.

So as you live your life, playing your own little scene in the great cosmic play, will you just lazily go through the motions? Or will you give it absolutely everything you've got - your full creativity, hard work, and passion - to make your scene the best it can possibly be?

If you choose to really go for it, your life's scene can be an inspiring, one-of-a-kind masterpiece that uplifts the entire play. It's up to you!

I'll leave you with one more inspiring thought: Re-dedicate yourself every day to perfect your act with love, creativity and service to others. It's up to you!

On one level, you'll feel satisfied achieving your goals. But on a bigger level, you'll be helping to make the entire grand drama more awesome and meaningful through your contributions.

When your time on stage eventually ends, your scene will be a lasting part of the infinite creative journey. It's your chance to let your unique talents blossom!

So every morning you get to choose: Will I just phone it in today? Or will I give this performance everything I've got to uplift the whole play?

The choice is yours each day. The stage is waiting for your full radiant participation!

Printed in Great Britain
by Amazon